THE GLENCOE LITERATURE LIBRARY

Winter Thunder

and

The Christmas of the Phonograph Records

with Related Readings

Glencoe
McGraw-Hill

New York, New York Columbus, Ohio Woodland Hills, California Peoria, Illinois

Acknowledgments

Grateful acknowledgment is given authors, publishers, photographers, museums, and agents for permission to reprint the following copyrighted material. Every effort has been made to determine copyright owners. In case of any omissions, the Publisher will be pleased to make suitable acknowledgments in future editions.

Winter Thunder by Mari Sandoz, copyright 1954 by Mari Sandoz. Reprinted by arrangement with the University of Nebraska Press.

The Christmas of the Phonograph Records A Recollection, by Mari Sandoz, copyright 1966 by the Estate of Mari Sandoz. Reprinted by arrangement with the University of Nebraska Press.

"April Rain Song" from *Collected Poems* by Langston Hughes. Copyright © 1994 by the Estate of Langston Hughes. Reprinted by permission of Alfred A. Knopf, a Division of Random House, Inc.

"Dust of Snow" from *The Poetry of Robert Frost*, edited by Edward Connery Lathem, copyright 1923, © 1969 by Henry Holt & Co., copyright 1951 by Robert Frost. Reprinted by permission of Henry Holt and Company, LLC.

"A New Window Display" from *El Bronx Remembered* by Nicholasa Mohr. Copyright © 1975 by Nicholasa Mohr. Used by permission of HarperCollins Publishers.

"Snowflake Bentley" by Ruth Wallace-Brodeur. Reprinted by permission of the author.

"Hanukkah Eve in Warsaw," from *Stories for Children* by Isaac Bashevis Singer. Copyright © 1984 by Isaac Bashevis Singer. Reprinted by permission of Farrar, Straus & Giroux, LLC.

NOTE: The characters in these selections are based on historical persons and actual events. Certain words, phrases, references, and situations may offend some readers.

Cover art: *The Very Dead of Winter.* Jo Barry (living). Print. Bankside Gallery, London/The Bridgeman Art Library.

Glencoe/McGraw-Hill

*A Division of The **McGraw·Hill** Companies*

Send all inquiries to:
Glencoe/McGraw-Hill
8787 Orion Place
Columbus, OH 43240

ISBN 0-07-825322-5
Printed in the United States of America
1 2 3 4 5 6 7 8 9 026 04 03 02 01

Contents

Winter Thunder

Mari Sandoz

To my niece Celia, daughter of Young Jules Sandoz,
who, with her pupils,
was lost and found in the blizzard of 1949

Winter Thunder

THE SNOW BEGAN QUIETLY THIS TIME, like an afterthought to the gray Sunday night. The moon almost broke through once, but toward daylight a little wind came up and started white curls, thin and lonesome, running over the old drifts left from the New Year storm. Gradually the snow thickened, until around eight thirty the two ruts of the winding trails were covered and undisturbed except down in the Lone Tree district, where an old yellow bus crawled heavily along, feeling out the ruts between the choppy sand hills.

As the wind rose the snow whipped against the posts of a ranch fence across the trail, and caked against the bus windows, shutting in the young faces pressed to the glass. The storm increased until all the air was a powdery white and every hill, every trace of road, was obliterated. The bus wavered and swayed in its direction, the tracks filling in close upon the wheels as they sought out the trail lost somewhere far back, and then finally grasped at any footing, until it looked like some great snowy, bewildered bug seen momentarily through the shifting wind. But it kept moving, hesitating here, stalling there in the deepening drifts, bucking heavily into them, drawing back to try once more while the chains spun out white fans that were lost in the driving snow which seemed almost as thick, as dense. Once the bus had to back down from a steep little patch that might have led into a storm-lost valley with a ranch house and warmth and shelter. It started doggedly around, slower now, but decisive, feeling cautiously for traction on the drifted hillside. Then the wheels began to slip, catch, then slip again, the bus tipping precariously in the push of the wind, a cry inside lost under the rising noise of the storm.

For a long time it seemed that the creeping bus could not be stopped. Even when all discernible direction or purpose was finally gone, it still moved, backing, starting again, this way and that, plowing the deepened slope, swaying, leaning until it seemed momentarily very tall and held from toppling only by the thickness of the flying snow. Once more a wheel caught and held under the thunder of the red-hot smoking exhaust. It slipped, and held again, but now the force of the wind was too great. For a moment the tilting bus seemed to lift. Then it pivoted into a slow skid and turned half around, broadside. Slowly it went over, almost as though without weight at all, settling lightly against a drift, to become a part of it at that thickening place where the white storm turned to snowbanks, lost except that there were frightening cries from inside, and a hiss of steam and smoke from the hot engine against the snow.

In a moment the door was forced outward, the wind catching a puff of smoke as dark, muffled heads pushed up and were white in an instant. They were children, mostly in snowsuits and in sheepskin coats, thrust down over the bus side, coughing and gasping as the force of the blizzard struck them, the older ones hunching their shoulders to shield themselves and some of the rest.

Once more the engine roared out and the upper back wheel spun on its side, free and foolish in its awkward caking of snow. Then the young woman who had handed the children down followed them, her sheepskin collar up about her head, her arms full of blankets and lunch boxes.

"You'll have to give it up, Chuck," she called back into the smoking interior. "Quick! Bring the rest of the lunches—"

With Chuck, sixteen and almost as tall as a man, beside her, Lecia Terry pushed the frightened huddle of children together and hurried them away downwind into the wall of storm. Once she tried to look back through the smother of snow, wishing that they might have taken the rope and shovel from the toolbox. But there was no time to dig for them on the under side now.

Back at the bus thick smoke was sliding out the door into the snow that swept along the side. Flames began to lick up under the leaning windows, the caking of ice suddenly running from them. The glass held one moment and burst, and the flames whipped out, torn away by the storm as the whole bus was suddenly a wet, shining yellow that blistered and browned with the heat. Then there was a dull explosion above the roar of the wind, and down the slope the fleeing little group heard it and thought they saw a dark fragment fly past overhead.

"Well, I guess that was the gas tank going," Chuck shouted as he tried to peer back under his shielding cap. But there was only the blizzard closed in around them, and the instinctive fear that these swift storms brought to all living creatures, particularly the young.

There was sobbing among the children now, a small one crying out, "Teacher! Teacher!" inside the thick scarf about her face, clutching for Lecia in her sudden panic.

"Sh-h, Joanie. I'm right here," the young woman soothed, drawing the six-year-old to her, looking around for the others, already so white that she could scarcely see them in the powdery storm.

"Bill, will you help Chuck pack all the lunches in two, three boxes, tight, so nothing gets lost? Maggie's big sirup bucket'll hold a lot. Throw all the empties away. We'll have to travel light—" she said, trying to make it sound a little like an old joke.

"My father will be coming for me soon—" the eight-year-old Olive said primly. "So you need not touch my lunch."

"Nobody can find us here," Chuck said shortly, and the girl did not reply, too polite to argue. But now one of the small boys began to cry. "I want my own lunch box too, Teacher," he protested, breathless from the wind. "I—I want to go home!"

His older brother slapped him across the ear muffs with a mittened hand. "Shut up, Fritz," he commanded. "You can't go home. The bus is—" Then he stopped, looking toward the teacher, almost lost only an arm's length away, and the full realization of their plight struck him. "We can't go home," he said, so quietly that he could scarcely be heard in the wind. "The bus is burned and Chuck and Miss Lecia don't know where we are—"

"Sure we know!" Chuck shouted against him without looking up from the lunch packing, his long back stooped protectively over his task. "Don't we know, Lecia? Anyway, it won't last. Radio this morning said just light snow flurries, or Dad wouldn't have let me take the bus out 'stead of him, even sick as he was." The tall boy straightened up, the lunch boxes strung to the belt of his sheepskin to bang together in the wind until they were snow-crusted. "Baldy Stever'll be out with his plane looking for his girl friend soon's it clears a little, won't he, Lecia?" he said. "Like he came New Year's, with skis on it."

But the bold talk did not quiet the sobbing, and the teacher's nod was lost in the storm as she tied scarves and mufflers across the faces of the younger children, leaving only little slits for the eyes, with the brows and lashes already furred with snow. Then she lined up the seven, mixing the ages from six-year-old Joanie to twelve-year-old Bill, who limped heavily as he moved in the deepening snow. One of the blankets she pinned around the thinly dressed Maggie, who had only a short outgrown coat, cotton stockings, and torn overshoes against the January storm. The other blanket she tied around herself, ready to carry Joanie on her back, Indian fashion, when the short little legs were worn out.

Awkwardly, one after another, Lecia pulled the left arm of each pupil from the sleeve, buttoned it inside the coat and then tied the empty sleeve to the right arm of the one ahead. She took the lead, with little Joanie tied to her belt, where she could be helped. Chuck was at the tail end of the clumsy little queue, just behind Bill with the steel-braced ankle.

"Never risk getting separated," Lecia remembered hearing her pioneer grandfather say when he told of burying the dead from the January blizzard of 1888 here, the one still called the school children's storm. "Never get separated and never stop moving until you find shelter—"

The teacher squinted back along the line, moving like some long snowy winter-logged animal, the segmented back bowed before the sharpening blizzard wind. Just the momentary turn into the storm took her breath and frightened her for these children hunched into themselves, half of them crying softly, hopelessly, as though already lost. They must hurry. With not a rock anywhere and not a tree within miles to show the directions, they had to seek out the landmark of the ranch country—the wire fence. So the girl started downwind again, breaking the new drifts as she searched for valley ground where fences were most likely, barbed-wire fences that might lead to a ranch, or nowhere except around some hay meadow. But it was their only chance the girl from the sand hills knew. Stumbling, floundering through the snow, she kept the awkward string moving, the eyes of the older ones straining through frozen lashes for even the top of one fence post, those of the small ones turned in upon their fear as the snow caked on the mufflers over their faces and they stumbled blindly to the pull from ahead.

Once there was a bolt of lightning, milky white in the blizzard, and a shaking of thunder, ominous winter thunder that stopped the moving feet. Almost at once the wind grew sharper, penetrating even Chuck's heavy sheepskin coat, numbing the ears and feet as panting, sobbing, the children plowed on again, the new drifts soon far above Lecia's boots, and no visibility, no way to avoid them.

With their hands so awkwardly useless, someone stumbled every few steps, but the first to fall was the crippled Bill, the others, the crying ones too, standing silent in the storm, not even able to slap one frozen hand against another while the boy was helped up. After that others went down, and soon it was all that the teacher and the boy Chuck could do to keep the children moving as they pushed through the chop hills and found themselves going up what seemed a long wind-swept, wind-frozen slope, Lecia carrying Joanie on her back most of the time now. But they kept moving somehow, barely noticing even the jack rabbit that burst out among their feet and was gone into the storm. Otherwise there was nothing.

After a long, long time they reached what seemed a high ridge of hills standing across the full blast of the north wind that bent them low and blinded. Suddenly Chuck's feet slid off sideways into a hole, a deep-cupped blowout hidden by the storm. Before he could stop, he had drawn the rest tumbling in after him, with an avalanche of snow. Crying, frightened, the smaller ones were set to their feet and brushed off a little. Then they all crouched together under the bank to catch their breath out of the wind, shivering, wet from the snow that had fallen inside their clothes, which were already freezing hard as board.

"With the blowouts always from the northwest to the southeast," Chuck shouted into the teacher's covered ear, "the wind's plainly from the north, so we're being pushed about due south. That direction there can't be a house for five, six miles, even if we could find it—unless we got clear out of our home country—"

The girl shivered, empty with fear. "—So that's why we haven't found a fence," she said slowly. "We're probably in the old Bar M summer range, miles and miles across. But we can't go any other direction—"

"I could alone; I could make it out alone!" Chuck shouted suddenly, angrily.

For a moment the teacher was silent, waiting, but when he added nothing more, she said: "You can't leave these little ones now, Chuck. Even if you were sure you could find a ranch—"

There was no reply, except that the crippled boy began to cry, a reddening from his ankle coming up through the snow that was packed into his overshoes around the brace. Others were sobbing too, and shaking with cold, but the younger ones were very quiet now, already drowsing, and so the young teacher had to get to her feet and help lift the children out of the blowout. Slapping the muffler-covered cheeks, shaking the smaller ones so hard that the caked snow fell from them, she got the line moving again, but very slowly. She was worn out too, from the path-breaking and with Joanie in her arms to warm the child, keep her from the sleep of freezing that came upon her on Lecia's back, with only the thin blanket against the ice of the wind.

They seemed to be going down now, through a long deep-drifted slope, plowing into buried yucca clumps, the sharp spears penetrating the snowsuits, even the boot tops. Here a few head of cattle passed them, less than three feet away and barely to be seen. They were running, snow-caked, blinded, bawling, and Lecia squinted anxiously back into the storm for others, for a herd that might be upon them, trample them as surely as stampeding buffaloes. But there were no more now, and she could see that Chuck was shouting, "Little chance of its clearing up soon, with that snow thunder and those cattle already drifting so fast—all that way from the winter range!"

Yes, drifting fast with the force and terror of the storm, even hardy, thick-haired range cattle running!

Then suddenly one of the younger boys cried out something. "Teacher!" he repeated, "I saw a post!"

But it must have been a trick of the wind, for there was only the driving snow, except that the sharp-eyed Maggie saw one too, ahead and to the right—a snowy post with only the upper foot or so out of the drifts, holding up a strand of gray wire taut and humming in the cold.

For a moment Lecia could not see through the blurring of her eyes. At least this was something to follow, but which way? To her signal Chuck lifted his arm and dropped it. He didn't recognize the fence either, and so the teacher took the easier direction, leftward, only side-face to the wind, although it might lead to the hills, to some final drift as the fleeing cattle would end.

Moving slowly along the fence, Lecia knew that it could not be much farther anyway. Her arms were wooden with cold and the weight of the child, her legs so weary in the deepening drifts that with each step it seemed that she could never lift a snow-caked boot again.

Then suddenly Chuck was doubling up the line. "I think I know where we are! That old split post just back there's where we made a take-down running coyotes with Dad's hounds this fall. If I'm right, this is Miller's north meadow, and there's a strip of willows down ahead there, off to the right—"

For a moment the girl set Joanie into the deep snow, panting, and even when she caught her breath, she was afraid to speak.

"How far to a house?" she finally asked, her lips frozen.

"There's no house along this fence if it's the Miller," Chuck had to admit. "It just goes around the meadow, three, four miles long."

"You're sure—" the teacher asked slowly, "—sure there's no cross fence to the ranch? You might get through, find help in time—"

The boy could only shake his snowy head and then, thinking that the storm hid this, he shouted the words on the wind. No, no cross fence, and the ranch was five miles south. Not even a haystack left in the valley here. Miller had had his hay balers in this fall, hauled it all out for his fancy Angus herd.

Then they must take a chance on the willows, with Bill hardly able to limp along, Joanie too heavy to carry, and several others worn out. So they wallowed through the drifted fence and tried to keep parallel to its direction, but far enough in the meadow to see any willows. There must be willows now.

Suddenly Lecia went down in what must have been a deep gully, the ground gone, the girl sinking into soft powdery snow to her shoulder. Panting, choking, she managed to get Joanie and the rest back out and the frightened ones quieted a little. Then she swung off right along the barer edge of the gully, seeking a place to cross. The wind was blowing in powerful gusts now, so that she could scarcely stand up. Bent low she dragged at the line behind her, most of the children crawling in the trench she plowed for them. There was no crying now—only the slow, slow moving. Perhaps they should dig into the snow here below the gully bank. Indians and trappers had done that and survived. But they had thick-furred buffalo robes to shut out the cold and snow, and they were grown men, tough, strong—not helpless, worn-out children, their frozen feet heavy as stone, with only an overgrown boy and a twenty-three-year-old girl to lead them, keep them alive.

More and more often Lecia had to stop, her head down, her arms dropping the weight of the little girl. But there seemed to be a shallowing in the gully now, and so it was time she tried to break a path through it and turned back toward the fence if they were not to wander lost as so many did that other time, long ago, when a teacher and her nine pupils were lost, finally falling to die on the prairie. They must cling to the fence here, if it went no farther than around the meadow. At least it was proof that something existed on the earth except the thick, stinging blizzard, with a white, freezing, plodding little queue caught in the heard of it, surrounded.

Once when the girl looked up from the running snow it seemed there was something darkish off to the right, little farther than arm's reach away. She saw it again, something rounded, perhaps a willow clump, low, snow filled, and possibly with more near by. Signaling to Chuck, Lecia turned down to it—a willow covered as in sleep, but with at least two more bushes just beyond, larger, darker, and standing closer together, their longer upper arms snow-weighted, entwined over the drifts. There, between the clumps, out of the worst of the storm, she left the children squatted close, the blankets held over them. With the belts of her coat and Chuck's, they tied the longer brushy tops of the two clumps together as solidly as they could. Then, fighting the grasping wind, they managed to fasten the blankets across the gap between the willows, to hold awhile. Behind this protection Lecia dug through the snow to the frozen ground while Chuck gathered dead wood. Inside a close little kneeling circle of children they built a fire pile with some dry inner bark and a piece of sandwich paper for the lighting. Awkwardly, with freezing hands the teacher and Chuck hurried, neither daring to think about matches, dry ones, in any pocket after this stumbling and falling through the snow.

The two smaller children were dropping into the heavy sleep of exhaustion and cold and had to be held in their places by the older ones while Chuck dug swiftly through his pockets, deeper, more awkwardly, then frantically, the circle of peering eyes like those of fearful young animals, cornered, winter-trapped.

Down to his shirt, Chuck found some in his pocket, six in a holder made of two rifle cartridges slipped together. Hurrying clumsily he struck one of the matches. It sputtered and went out, the flames sucked away. They had to try again, making a closer circle, with the coattails of the children thrown up over their heads to shut out the storm. This time the match caught on the waxed paper and the diamond willow began to snap and sizzle in the snow, throwing a dancing light up to the circle of crouching children.

But it seemed even colder now that they had stopped walking and Lecia thought of the night ahead, with the temperature surely down to twenty-five or thirty below zero. Beyond that she would not look now; but to get through this night they must have a great pile of wood, and they must have shelter even to hold a fire.

"We can't both go out at one time," the teacher told Chuck in their planning, somehow making it seem as for a long, long time. "It's too risky for the children. We might not get back."

The boy looked around from the fire he was nursing, and upward, but there was still no thinning of the storm, the area of snowy visibility almost as small as the confines of their new meat-freeze room at the ranch. Even so he gave the girl no sign of agreement.

Lecia set willow poles into the snowbanks as she went to look for wood, none farther apart than the outstretched reach of her arms. She found more willows, each clump sitting alone in the isolation of the driving storm, so cold now that the green wood snapped off like glass. Each time it was only by the row of sticks in the drifts that she managed to stagger her blinded and panting way back against the wind with her load of wood.

The brushier portions she piled behind the blankets of the shelter to catch the snow and shut out the wind. Some, long as fish poles, she pushed through the willow clumps and across the opening between, in a sort of lattice inside the bellying blankets that Eddie and Calla tried to hold in place. They were the first of the children to separate themselves from the snowy composite, the enforced co-ordinate that had been the queue driven by the storm, the circle that shielded the sprouting fire. Now they were once more individuals who could move alone, hold the blankets from blowing inward, pile the dry powdery snow from the ground against and between the sticks, trying to work it like plaster, building a wall between the clumps of willows. Even Bill helped a little, as far as he could reach without moving the bad ankle. They worked slowly, clumsily, pounding their freezing hands at the fire, but returning.

By one o'clock the north wind was cut off so that the fire fattened and burned higher, softening the ice cake to the clothing until it could be knocked off, and softening the face of the drift reached by the wind-blown heat. The children packed this against the north wall too, and into the willow clumps both ways, drawing the rounded wall inward toward the top along the bend of the willows, making what looked like half of an Indian snow shelter, or the wickiup Calla had seen at the county fair, just high enough at the center for a seven-year-old to stand up, the snow walls glistening rosy in the firelight as the wind was shut off.

"That's a good job!" Chuck shouted over the roar of the storm as he tried to rub circulation into Joanie's waxen feet. The small girl was beginning to cry out of her sleep with the first pain; others began too, their ears and hands swollen and purpling, their toes painful as their boots thawed. But it seemed that the feet of nine-year-old Maggie must be lost, the ragged old overshoes and cotton stockings so frozen that she had to cut them away with Eddie's knife. Under them her feet were like stone, dead white stone, although the girl was working hard to rub life into them. She worked silently and alone, as had become natural long ago, her thin face pinched and anxious with the pain and the alarm.

Of them all only Olive seemed untouched. She was dry in her heavy waterproofed snowsuit with attached rubber feet inside the snow boots. And she was still certain that her father would soon come for her.

"He would not care to leave me in such an unpleasant place—"

When they had the semicircular wall of the shelter drawn in as far as the snow would hold, Lecia decided to pull the blankets away from the outside and use one over the top, with the belt-tied willows sticking through a smoke hole cut in the center. But as the blankets came down, part of the loose snow wall was blown in by the force of the blizzard, the huddle of children suddenly white again, the fire almost smothered. So the wall had to be rebuilt in discouragement, but with care, using more brush and sticks, more fire-softened snow to freeze in place as soon as it was struck by the storm. Lecia had to stop several times for her hands too, pounding them hard, holding them over the fire, the diamond sparkling. She tried to turn the ring off before the swelling became too great and then gave it up. The wall must be finished, and when it was solid, Calla came to whisper under the roar of the wind. "Bill's been eating the lunch," she said.

"Oh, Bill! That's not fair to the others, to your own little sister, Joanie!" Lecia cried. Suddenly not the good teacher, she grabbed up the containers and hung them on high branches out in plain sight for watching, for reminders and derision from the other children. "Why, it may be days before we are found!" she scolded, in her exasperation saying what should have been kept hidden in silence.

Before the boy could defend himself with a plea of hunger or his usual complaint about the crippled foot, some realization of their plight had struck the others. Even little Fritz, with the security of an older sister and brother like Calla and Eddie along, began to sob. Only the round-cheeked Olive was calm, the others angered to see it, wanting to shout against her outsider's assurance, to tell her she was too stupid and green to know that her father could not come for her in such a blizzard, that he would never find her if he could get through. But they were silent under the teacher's admonitory eye. And, as in the schoolhouse and on the playground, Bill had withdrawn, except that now it could not be more than a foot or two.

As the frozen earth between the willow humps became soggy, Calla and Eddie helped move the others around so that there was room to draw the fire first one way and then another, to dry and warm the ground. Lecia watched to see that they set no one afire and then bowed her head out into the storm again. Chuck was dragging in willows for the night. They drove sticks into the hardening drifts around the front of the shelter and piled brush against them to catch the snow. It filled in as fast as they worked until there was no more than a little crawling hole left. Then Chuck laid a mat of brushy sticks on the ground and packed soft snow into them to freeze, making a handled slab big enough to close the low doorway. Now, so long as the blanket with the smoke hole stayed tied over the top they could be as warm as they wished in the little shelter that was scarcely longer than a tall man—a close cramping for the teacher, Chuck, and the seven pupils, but easily warmed with a few fingers of wood, an Indian fire. Safe and warm so long as the shelter stood against the rising ferocity of the blizzard, and the willows lasted.

By now the cold stung the nose and burned the lungs, the snow turned the sharp crystals that drew blood from the bare skin. It drove the teacher and Chuck in to the fire, shaking, unable, it seemed, ever to be warmed through again. Lecia opened her sheepskin coat, hung up her frozen scarf and cap and shook out her thick brown hair that gleamed in the firelight. Even with her tawny skin red and swollen, her gold-flecked hazel eyes blood-shot, she was still a pretty girl, and the diamond on her hand flashed as she hunted for her stick of white salve to pass around for the raw, bleeding lips. It was all she could do.

Now they tried to plan for what was to come, but here they were as blind as in the flight through the storm. There would be sickness, with the noses already running, Joanie coughing deep from her chest, and, worst of all, Maggie's feet that seemed to be dying. Besides, the fire must be kept going and the food spread over three, perhaps four, days.

Here Bill raised his complaining voice, "You ain't our boss outside of school! We'll do what we want to. There ain't enough to eat for everybody."

"You mean *isn't*, not *ain't*," the teacher corrected firmly. "And talking like that—when you've barely missed one lunch time!"

"You ain't never my boss," Chuck said casually, "—only about the kids while in the bus, like you do with my dad when he's driving. I sure can do what I want to here, and I'll do it."

Slowly the girl looked around the ring of drowsy, firelit eyes upon her, some uneasy at this bold talk to their teacher, but some smaller ones aping the defiance of the big boys. Chuck, who sat almost a head taller than Lecia, grinned down at the pretty young teacher but with an arrogance that was intended to remind her he saw nothing here as his responsibility, nothing this side of the bus except saving himself.

Unable to reply in words that would not frighten the children more, the teacher looked past the fire into the boy's broad, defiant face, into his unblinking, storm-red eyes, the look commanding at first, then changing to something else in spite of herself, into a sort of public test, until it seemed she dared not turn her gaze away or at that instant the sixteen-year-old boy must assert his victory by plunging out into the storm and perhaps destroy himself, perhaps bring death to all of them.

Before this silent, incomprehensible struggle the children were uneasy and afraid, even the coughing stilled, so that the storm seemed very loud outside the smoke hole. But little Fritz was too young to be held so for long. "I'm hungry!" he shouted against the restraining hand of his sister. "I want my lunch!"

As though freed, released, Chuck sat back and grinned a little at the small boy. Matter of factly the teacher washed her raw hands with snow and held them over the fire. Then she spread her napkin on her lap and set out all there was in the eight lunches now: fourteen sandwiches, most of them large, six pieces of Sunday cake, a handful of cookies, a few pieces of candy, and six apples and two oranges, frozen hard. There were two thermos bottles of milk, and these Lecia pushed away into the snow wall.

"If somebody gets sick and can't eat solid food," she said to the owners, their eyes following her hands in consternation. Even with the best management, there would be no food of any kind in a few days, but this the small owners could not yet understand.

The frozen fruit she handed to Chuck and, without meeting the girl's eyes, he set it around the coals for toasting, to be eaten now because it would not keep well, and might sicken leaner stomachs. In the meantime Lecia set one lunch box filled with snow near the fire and packed away all except four of the big sandwiches into the others, the eyes of the children following her hands here too, even as she hung the containers back above her head. Then she divided the four sandwiches into halves and passed them around.

"Eat very slowly," she cautioned. "Blizzards usually last three days, so we must make what we have here last too, probably clear to Thursday, or longer."

But Bill seemed not to be listening. "Chuck's eating!" he suddenly protested. "He ain't, *isn't*, in on the lunches."

For a moment the teacher looked sternly at the boy. "After Chuck carried them all from the bus, helped you through the bad places, and helped to make the shelter and the fire!" the girl said in astonishment. "Now we'll have no more of this bickering and complaint. Here we are equal partners, and not one of us will get out of this alive unless we keep working together. Even your comic books should have taught you that much! And don't think this is play. You remember what the storm of 1888 was called in your history book—because so many school children died in it. That storm was short, not over two days most places, nothing for length like the one we had holiday time this year, and no telling about this one. Most of the children in 1888 died because somebody got panicky, didn't think, or they didn't stick together—"

There was silence all around the fire now, the storm seeming to rise, the children edging closer to each other, glancing fearfully over their shoulders as though toward night windows with terrible things stalking outside.

"Oh, we're O.K.," Chuck said optimistically. "We can last three days easy here—" the rebellion gone from him, or hidden for the moment.

Thinking of a five-day storm, the teacher looked around the frightened, sooty faces, the children coughing and sniffling, their pocket tissue gone, the few handkerchiefs hung to dry and wondered if any, even the man-tall Chuck, would be here by then.

But Olive, the newcomer, was unconcerned. "I should like another sandwich, Miss Terry. From my own lunch, please," she said, with the formality of an old-fashioned boarding school for eight-year-olds. "I won't need the remainder. My father will come for me when it is time."

"He won't find you—" Maggie said as she rubbed at her feet, color seeping into them now, an angry gray-splotched purple, with pain that twisted the thin face.

"My father will come," Olive repeated, plainly meaning that he was not like the fathers of the others here, particularly Maggie's, who had done nothing since the war except make a little South Pacific bug juice, as he called it, for himself from chokecherries, wild grapes, or raisins in the way they did in the war. He had only a little piece of copper tubing, and so he couldn't make more than enough for himself, yet he got into jail just the same, for crashing his old truck through the window of the county assistance office. But things had not been good before that. Often this fall Maggie was at school when the bus arrived, not waiting at the stop near their crumbling old sod shack but walking the three miles. Sometimes her face was bruised, but she was silent to any questioning. If Maggie lost her feet now, it was because she had no warm snowsuit and high boots like the others, only the short old coat above her skinny knees, the broken overshoes with the soles flopping.

But there was still a cheerful face at the fire. Although little Fritz's cheeks seemed swollen to bursting and his frosted ears stood away under the flaps of his cap, he could still show his gap-toothed grin in mischief.

"If we don't get home till Thursday, Teacher, Baldy'll be awful mad at you when he comes flying out Wednesday—"

The rest laughed a little, drowsily. "Maybe Baldy won't be flying around that soon," Eddie said, and was corrected by Calla's sisterly concern. "Don't say Baldy. Say Mr. Stever."

But the teacher busied herself hanging up everything loose. Then with Chuck's knife she slit the remaining blanket down the middle and fastened half around each side against the snow wall, like a tipi lining. By the time the white blizzard darkness came, the smaller children had all been taken outside for the last time and lay in fretful, uneasy sleep. Olive had been the last, waiting stubbornly for her father until she toppled forward. Calla caught her and made room for the girl still murmuring, "Papa—"

Finally the last sob for parent and home was stilled, even Joanie asleep, her feverish head in the teacher's lap, her throat raw and swelling, with nothing except hot snow water to ease the hollow cough. There were half a dozen lozenges in Lecia's pocket but these must be saved for the worse time that would surely come.

The children were packed around the fire like little pigs or puppies on a very cold night. Chuck was at the opposite side from Lecia, the boys on his side, the girls on hers, with Calla and her brothers around the back. The older ones lay nearer the wall, their arms over the younger to hold their restlessness from the fire.

But Bill was still up, drawn back under the willows, his heap pulled into his sheepskin collar, his ankle bent to him. He watched the teacher doze in fatigue, met her guilty waking gaze sullenly. But finally he reached down into his pocket and drew out something in waxed paper.

"I didn't eat the piece you gave me—" he said, holding out his half of the sandwich.

"Bill! That was fine of you," the girl said, too worn out for more as she reached up to put it away.

"No—no, you eat it. I guess you didn't take any."

A moment Lecia looked at the boy, but he avoided her as he edged himself around Chuck closer to the fire, turning his chilled back to the coals, and so she ate the buttered bread with the thick slice of strengthening cold beef, while more snow was driven in through the smoke hole and settled in sparkling dust toward the little fire. There were white flashes too, and the far rumble of winter thunder.

"Is—is there lots of willows left?" the crippled boy asked.

The teacher knew what he meant—how many clumps, and if so far out that someone might let lost.

"I think there are quite a few," she replied, needing to reassure the boy, but unable to make it a flat lie.

A long time he sat silent. Finally he pulled his cap off and shook the long yellowish hair back from his petulant face. "I wonder what Mother's doing—" he said slowly, looking away, his hand seeking out the tortured ankle. Lecia motioned him to hold it over to her and so she did not need to reply, to ask what all the mothers of these children must be doing, with the telephone lines still down from the other storm and surely nobody foolish enough to try bucking this one, unless it might be Olive's father, the new Eastern owner of the little Box Y ranch.

With snow water heated in the lunch tin, Lecia washed the poor stick that was the boy's ankle, gently sponging the bone laid almost bare where the frozen snow and the iron brace wore through the scarred and unhealthy skin.

"It looks pretty bad, Bill, but you probably won't have to put the brace on for days—" Lecia started to comfort, but it was too late, and she had to see fear and anger and self-pity darken the face in the firelight. Because nothing could be unsaid, the girl silently bandaged the ankle with half of the boy's handkerchief. "Now get a little sleep if you can," she said gently.

The boy crawled in next to Eddie as though Ed were the older, and for a long time the teacher felt the dark eyes staring at her out of the shadowy coat collar as though she had deliberately maneuvered this plunge into the blizzard.

Several times before midnight the girl started to doze but jerked herself awake at the frozen creak of the willow shelter, to push the out-tossed arms back and replenish the fire.

Eddie's cough began to boom deep as from a barrel. He turned and moaned, digging at his chest, Calla helpless beside him, her sleep-weighted eyes anxious on the teacher. Maggie too was finally crying now. Her feet had puffed up and purpled dark as jelly bags, with the graying spots that would surely break and slough off, perhaps spread in gangrene. Yet all Lecia could do was turn the girl's feet from the fire and push them behind the blanket against the snow to relieve the pain and itching a little. Perhaps only freeze them more. Lecia touched the girl's forehead to calm her but felt her stiffen and start to pull away this unaccustomed kindly touch. Then Maggie relaxed a little and as the teacher stroked the hot temples, she wondered how many days it might be before help could get through. Suddenly their plight here seemed so hopeless, the strength and wisdom of her twenty-three years so weak and futile, that she had to slip out into the storm for calm. And finally Maggie slept, worn out, but still tearing at her feet.

To the weary girl watching, half asleep, at the fire, the roar of the storm rose and fell like the panting of a great live thing, sometimes a little like many great planes warming up together. If only she had married Dale Stever New Year's, they would be in the Caribbean now, these children all safe at home, with probably no other teacher available so soon. Once Lecia turned her swollen hand to the fire, watching the ring catch and break the light into life, and tried to recall the fine plans Dale had made for them. He wasn't a rancher's son like those who usually took her to parties and dances—like Joe, or Wilmo, or even Ben, of the local bank. Dale had come from outside last summer and bought up the sale pavilion in town. Since then he flew all around the surrounding ranch country in a plane the color of a wild canary rising from a plum thicket, gathering stock for the sales. Fairtime he took Lecia and her friend Sallie down to the state fair, and several times on long trips since, to Omaha to the ballet and to Denver. At first it seemed he was all jolly big-talk, with windy stories of his stock in an oil company down in Dallas and in a Chicago commission house. He had a touch of gray at his temples that he thought made him look distinguished when he had his hat on, and to their fathers he called himself the Dutch uncle of the two girls. But gradually he concentrated on Lecia, and at Christmas there was the big diamond and the plane ready to fly south. He even took her to the school board to ask for a release from her contract.

"No," the old school director told the girl. "Bill Terry was a friend of mine, brought me into the country. I can't help his granddaughter marry no man in a rush hurry."

Dale laughed confidently and put his arm about the girl's shoulder as they left, but somehow Lecia couldn't break her contract. They must wait until school was out. Dale had been angry. "This is no life for a girl as pretty as you," he said. Truly he was right. Today it was no life for any girl.

Soon after midnight Lecia was startled out of a doze by the sound of cattle bawling somewhere in the roar of the storm, like the herds that passed her home in the night of the May blizzard three years ago, when so many died in the drifts and lakes that the whole region was a stench far into the summer. Then suddenly the girl realized where she was, and hurried bareheaded out into the storm. The bawling was very close; any moment hundreds of storm-blinded cattle might be running over the little willows, over their own two clumps.

Lecia dragged burning sticks from the fire, but in an instant the storm had sucked their flame away. So, with her arms up to shield her eyes from the snow that was sharp as steel dust, she stood behind the shelter shouting the "Hi-ah! Hi-ah!" she had learned when she helped the cowboys push cattle to market. It was a futile, lost little sound against cattle compelled to run by an instinct that could not be denied, compelled to flee for survival before the descent of the arctic storm, never stopping until trapped in some drift, or boldly overtaken in some open fence corner to freeze on their feet, as Lecia had seen them stand.

Realizing her danger as a warmth crept over her, the girl stumbled back into the shelter and crouched at the fire. She barely noticed the sting of returning blood in her ears and face while she listened until the drifting herd was surely past, made more afraid by the knowledge of this thing that drove cattle galloping through the night, the power of it, and how easily it could overcome the little circle of children here if it were not for the handful of fire, for the walls of the storm's own snow.

Toward morning the weary girl knew that she could not keep awake. She had stirred Chuck to sit up a while, but he was unable to shake off the weight of sleep so heavy on an overgrown boy. Trying to remember how the Indians carried their fire—something about moss and damp, rotted wood—Lecia pulled old dead roots from the willow butts and laid them into the coals with the ends sticking far out. Even with waxed paper handy it would be a desperate chance. Willows burned fast as kindlings and there were only five matches, including the one from Eddie's pocket, and no telling how many spoiled by dampness.

Even so it was sweet to let herself sink into darkness, but it seemed that she awoke at once, stiff and cold from the nightmare that reached into the waking black, even the ashes of the fire spot cold. With the waxed paper held ready, the girl blew on the ends of the unburnt roots her hands found, carefully, breathless in her fear. At last a red spark glowed deep in one, and when the fire was going again, she slipped outside for calm in the cold that was like thin, sharp glass in the nose.

There was still no earth and no sky, only the white storm of late dawn blowing hard. But the wood had lasted and now Lecia put on a few extra sticks and heated water to wash the goose mush from the inflamed eyes of the children. She started a rousing song: "Get up! Get up, you sleepyhead!" but even before it was done, Joanie began to whimper, "I'm hungry—"

So the teacher laid out four sandwiches on sticks over the coals and then added another half for herself when she saw Bill watching. "There won't be anything more today except a pinch of cake unless the sun breaks through."

"If it does, we can stomp out a message on the snow," Calla said cheerfully.

"Yes, even if people can't travel for a whole week, Baldy'll come flying over to see about his girl friend," Bill said, boldly.

The younger boys laughed a little, but Chuck was more serious. "If the sky lightens at all and there's no blowing, I'll do the stomping before I leave."

"You'd run away now?" the teacher asked softly as she combed at Joanie's fine hair.

"Somebody's got to get help," he defended in loud words.

The children around the fire were suddenly quiet, turning their eyes to follow the tall boy as he pulled up his sheepskin collar and crawled out into the storm. And silent a long time afterward—all except Joanie, who sobbed softly, without understanding. Even Olive looked up once, but Maggie grated her feet hard along the snow wall and tore at their congestion as though she heard nothing.

Then suddenly there was stomping outside and Chuck came back in, snowy, thick frost all over his collar and cap, his brows and lashes in ice, the children pushing over toward him as to one gone, lost. He brought more wood, and the teacher seemed to have forgotten that he had said anything about leaving. But the children watched him now, even when they pretended they didn't, and watched Lecia too, for suspicion had come in.

The teacher started as for a school day, except that the arithmetic was rote learning of addition and multiplication tables and a quick run through some trick problems: "If I had a fox, a goose, and some corn to get across a river in a boat—" and then, "If I had a dollar to buy a hundred eggs—no, I should take something that won't make us hungry."

"Like a hundred pencils?"

"Well, yes, let's take pencils. I want to buy a hundred for a dollar. Some are five cents each, poor ones two and a half cents, and broken ones half a cent. How many of each kind must I buy?"

In history and nature study they talked about the Indians that still roamed the sand hills when Lecia's grandfather came into the country. They lived the winter long in skin tipis something like the shelter here, and almost as crowded, but with piles of thick-furred buffalo robes for the ground and the beds. The girls sat on one side, the boys on the other.

"Like we are here—" Fritz said, his eyes shining in the discovery. "We're Indians. Whoo-oo-oo!" he cried, slapping his mouth with his palm.

They talked about the food too, the piles of dried and pounded meat, the winter hunts, how the village and lodges were governed, and what the children did, their winter games, one almost like "button, button." The boys learned from the men—such things as arrow-making, and later bullet-making, hunting, fighting; and particularly the virtues of resourcefulness, courage, fortitude, and responsibility for all the people. A girl learned from the women—beading, tanning hides, and all the other things needed to live well with modesty, steadfastness, and generosity, and with courage and fortitude and responsibility too, for it was thought that the future of the people lay in the palms of women, to be cherished or thrown away.

"What does that mean, Teacher?" Fritz asked, hitting out in mischief at his brother Eddie, despite Calla and the teacher both watching, then shouting he was hungry again.

The rest tried to laugh a little as Calla whispered to her small brother, trying to make herself heard against the storm, while Lecia taught them a poem about Indians. Even Joanie repeated a few lines for her, although the child leaned weak and feverish against Calla while Bill comforted his bound ankle and Maggie tried hard to pull herself out of the curious drowsiness that had the teacher frightened.

After a while the children played "button, button," and tried to tell each other poems. When Eddie got stuck on "Snowbound," Bill nudged Fritz and they laughed as easily at his discomfiture as at school, perhaps because Chuck was back and this was the second day of the storm, with tomorrow the third. Then it would clear up and somebody with a scoop shovel would get his horse along the barer ridges to a telephone.

"Maybe somebody'll just come running over the hills to find us," Eddie teased, looking at Olive, turning his face from the teacher.

Well, even if nobody came and Baldy couldn't find a place to land with skis on his plane, he would have sacks of food and blankets and stuff dropped like in the movies and the newspapers.

"I saw it in a movie once, I did," Joanie cried.

So they talked, pretending no one was looking up at the hanging lunch buckets, or sick and afraid. But Lecia did not hear them.

"Oh-oo, Teacher's sleeping like one of those old Indian women up to Gordon, just sitting there!' Eddie exclaimed.

"Sh-h," Calla said, in her way. "Let her stretch out here," and with a polite smile Olive moved aside.

That night Joanie was delirious, and once Maggie slipped past the teacher out into the storm to relieve the fire of her feet. By midnight she couldn't stand on them, and the grayish spots were yellow under the thick skin of a barefoot summer, the swelling creeping above the girl's thin ankles, with red streaks reaching almost to the knees. Her eyes glistened, her cheeks were burning, and she talked of wild and dreadful things.

Lecia tried to remember all that she had read of frostbite, all that her grandfather had told, but she knew that the inflammation spreading past the frozen area was like the cold overtaking the fleeing cattle, and she had to make a desperate decision. She dug two holes deep into the snow wall and laid Maggie with her feet in them almost to her knees, wishing they had something waterproof for covering. The cold would probably freeze the girl more, but it would numb the nerves and perhaps slow the congestion and tissue starvation. Later, when the girl was restless again and crying, Lecia found the yellow spots spreading, painful and hard as boils. She burned the end of a safety pin and while Maggie's frightened eyes became caverns in her thin face, Lecia opened one of the spots. Bloody pus burst down over her hand. Holding the foot aside she wiped it away on the snow, from her ring too, and then slipped it from her shrunken finger and hung it on a twig overhead, where it swayed a little, like a morning dewdrop while she opened the rest of the festering.

While the girl's feet were bathed and bound in the sleeves torn from Lecia's white shirt blouse, she thrust them back into the snow. Then she gave Maggie half a cup of milk, very quietly, hoping none would awaken to see, although none needed it more. Almost at once the girl was asleep, to rest until the pus gathered again. But the first time Lecia returned with firewood she saw the thermos bottle half out. She jerked it from the hole. The milk was all gone, and across the little fire Olive stared at her teacher.

"It was mine," the girl said flatly.

So the time had come when the little food left must be hidden. Now, with all but Olive sleeping, was the time. When Lecia came back in, the girl held out something—the ring that had been left hanging on the twig and forgotten.

The next day and the next were the same, only colder, the drifts deeper and harder along the willows, the wind so sharp with snow that it froze the eyeballs. Lecia and Chuck covered their faces as they fought their way back against it, the wood dragging from their shoulders, tied by a strap of cloth cut off around the bottom of Lecia's coat. One at a time they went out and came back, a hand stretched ahead feeling for the next guide pole in the snow before the other let go of the last, the covered face turned from the storm to save the breath from being torn away by the wind.

All the third day there was watching out of the smoke hole for the sky that never appeared. When night finally came without star or stillness, even Lecia, who had tried to prepare herself for this eventuality, felt that she could not face another day of blizzard. Maggie no longer sat up now and both Joanie and Eddie were so sick—their fever high, their chests filling—that the teacher had to try something. She seemed to remember that the early settlers used willow bark to break a fever, so she steeped a handful in Maggie's tin cup until the liquid was strong and dark. She made the two children drink it, first experimentally then more, and after a while they began to sweat. When they awoke they were wet, their hair clinging to their vulnerable young foreheads, but they seemed better all the next day, except weak. Then at night it was the same with Joanie.

The fourth day was like the rest, colder, with the same white storm outside, the children hunching silent upon themselves inside. Sometimes a small one sobbed a little in sickness and hunger, but it was no more than a soft moaning now, even when Lecia divided most of the little food that was left. The children, even Chuck, took it like animals, and then sat silent again, the deep-socketed eyes watching, some slyly gnawing at willow sticks and roots hidden in the palm.

Everybody around the fire was coughing and fevered now, it seemed to Lecia, the bickering going beyond childish things to quarrels about real or fancied animosities between their families. Once even Calla spoke angrily to Bill, defending her brothers.

"At least they aren't mama babies like you!"

"Mama babies! I wouldn't talk if everybody knew that my family got a start in cattle by stealing calves—"

"You can't say such things!" Calla cried, up and reaching for Bill, caught without his brace and unable to flee into the storm, Joanie crying: "Don't! Don't hit my brother!"

When Lecia returned, Chuck was holding the two apart, shaking them both. The teacher spoke in anger and impatience too now, and Bill's face flushed with embarrassment and shame, the sudden red like fever in his hunger-grayed cheeks.

Only Maggie with her poor feet was quiet, and Olive, sitting as though stunned or somewhere far away. The teacher knew that she should do something for this girl, only eight yet apparently so self-contained. Olive never spoke of her father now, as none of the boys teased Lecia about Baldy any more. Olive was as remote about him as everything else since the night she drank the milk, and found the ring on a twig.

Too weary to think about it, and knowing she must keep awake in the night, Lecia stretched out for a nap. When she awoke Olive was sitting exactly the same, but the places of Chuck and Eddie were empty—Eddie out in the blizzard after his night of sweating. When the boys returned with wood, weak, dragging, almost frozen, and with something that Lecia had to be told outside. There seemed only one willow clump left.

One clump? Then they must start digging at the frozen butts, or even pull down their shelter to keep the fire alive, for now the boys too were believing that the storm would blow forever. Yet toward evening there was a thinning above the smoke hole, the sun suddenly there like a thin disk of milky ice from the bottom of a cup. It was almost a promise, even though the storm swept the sun away in a few minutes and the wind shifted around to the south, whipping in past the block the boys had in the hole of the shelter. The children shivered, restless. Once Eddie rose from his sleep and fought to get out, go home. When he finally awakened, he lay down in a chill, very close to the fire, and would not move until a stench of burning cloth helped rouse him. Then he drank the bitter willow bark tea too and finally he slept.

Friday morning the sun came out again toward ten o'clock, the same cold, pale disk, with the snow still running along the earth, running higher than the shelter or Chuck, shutting out everything except the veiled sun. The boy came in, looked around the starved, listless circle at the fire, at the teacher too, with her face that had been so pretty Monday morning gaunt and sooty now.

He laid two red-tipped matches, half of all he had, in the girl's lap. "I'm getting out," he said, and without a protest from anyone crawled through the hole and was gone.

The children were almost past noticing his desertion now, barely replying when spoken to. If the colds got worse or pneumonia struck, it would be over in a few hours. Maggie hadn't sat up since yesterday, lying flat, staring at the white storm blowing thin above the smoke hole. If any of them wondered how Lecia could keep the fire going alone, with nothing much except the willow butts left, none spoke of it. The teacher sat with her arms hanging between her knees, hopeless.

She finally stirred and put the matches away in waxed paper in her shirt pocket where her ring lay, buttoning the flap down carefully now. Joanie started to cough again, choking, turned red and then very white under the grime and grayness of her face, lying very still. Now Bill made the first gesture toward his small sister.

"Come here, Doll," he said gently, drawing her awkwardly from Lecia's lap, the child lifting her head slowly, holding herself away, looking up at him as a baby might at a stranger, to be weighed and considered. Then she snuggled against him and in a moment she was asleep.

After a long time there seemed a dull sound outside, and then Chuck was suddenly back, crawling in almost as though he had not left, panting in his weakness from the fight against the wind that had turned north again, and colder.

"Scared an eagle off a drift out there," he finally managed to say. "And there's a critter stuck in the snow—beyond the far willows. Small spring calf. Froze hard, but it's meat—"

Then the realization that Chuck was back struck the teacher. She was not alone with the children, and he too was safe for now. But there was something more. The boy who had resented them and his involvement in their plight—he had escaped and come back.

"Oh, Chuck!" the girl exclaimed. Then what he said reached her mind. "A calf? Maybe we could build a fire there so we can cut some off, if we can't get it all out." She reached for her boots. "But we'll have to go work at it one at a time—" looking around the firelit faces that were turned toward her as before, but the eyes alert, watching as though a morsel might be dropped, even thrown.

"I'll go with Chuck, Miss Lecia," Bill said softly. "He can show me and I'll show you. Save time hunting—"

The teacher looked at the crippled boy, already setting Joanie gently aside and reaching for his brace. She felt pride in him, and unfortunate doubt.

"He can probably make it," Chuck said, a little condescending. "It's not over an eighth of a mile, and I found more willows farther along the way, the drifts mostly frozen hard too. I blazed the willows beyond our poles—"

"You'll be careful—mark everything," the girl pleaded.

"We've got to. It's snowing again, and the sun's gone."

It seemed hours since the boys went out and finally the teacher had to go after them, appalled that the younger ones had to be left alone, yet it must be done. She moved very carefully, feeling her way in the new storm, going sideways to it, from pole to pole. Then she came to a place where the markers were gone, probably blown down and buried by the turning wind. The boys were out there, lost, in at least fifteen, perhaps twenty, below zero. Without sticks to guide her way back, the girl dared go no farther but she crouched there, bowed before the wind, cupping her mouth with her mittens, shouting her hopeless: "Boys! Chuck! O-hoo!" the wind snatching it away. She kept calling until she was shaking and frozen and then to a frightening warmth.

But now she had to keep on, for it seemed that she heard something, a vague, smothered sound, and yet a little like a reply. Tears freezing on her face she called again and again until suddenly the boys were at her feet, there before she could see them, so much like the snow, like white dragging animals, one bowed, half carrying the other. For a few minutes they crouched together in desperate relief, the snow running over them as something immovable, like an old willow butt. Then, together, they pulled themselves up and started back. When they finally reached the shelter, out of breath and frozen, they said nothing of what had happened, nor spoke at all for a while. Yet all, even little Joanie, seemed to sense that the boys had almost been lost.

As soon as the teacher was warmed a little, she started out alone, not certain that she could make it against the storm, but knowing that she must try to get meat. She took Chuck's knife, some dry bark, waxed paper, the two matches in her shirt pocket, and a bundle of poles pulled from their shelter. Moving very carefully beyond the gap in the willow markers, she set new sticks deep, and tipped carefully with the new storm. She found the farther willow clumps with Chuck's blazing, and the brush pile the boys had made, and beside it the ice-covered head of the calf still reaching out of the snow. The hole they had dug around the red hindquarters was drifted in loosely but easily dug out. Lecia set a fire pile there and felt for a match with her numb fingers, fishing in the depths of her pocket, something round in the way, her ring. But she got the match and lighted the fire under her shielding sheepskin coat. For a long time she crouched protectively over the flame, the wind carrying away the stench of burning calf hair. As the skin thawed, she hacked at it the way Indians must have done here a thousand years ago, their stone knives sharper and more expertly handled.

At a sound she looked over her shoulder and saw a coyote not three feet away, gaunt-bellied too, and apparently no more afraid than a hungry dog. But suddenly he caught the human smell, even against the wind, and was gone. He would have made a soft rug at the fire, Lecia thought, and wondered if he might not return to watch just beyond the wall of storm. But she was too busy to look. As the heat penetrated the meat, she cut off one slice after another until she had a little smoky pile, not much for nine people who had lived five days on one lunch apiece, but enough to bring tears that were not all from the storm. In this meat, perhaps three pounds, might lie the life of her pupils.

Lecia scattered the fresh ashes over the calf to keep the coyotes away and piled brush into the fire hole. Then she headed sideways into the storm, so violent that it was a good thing she had the strength of a little cautious meat inside her, for it seemed no one could face the wounding snow. Numb and frightened, she managed to hold herself, not get hurried, panicked, never move until the next broken willow, the next marker was located. So she got back, to find Chuck out near the shelter digging wood from the old clumps, watching, uneasy.

It was hard for the children to wait while the thinner slices of meat roasted around the sticks. When the smell filled the little shelter, Lecia passed out toasted bits to be chewed very slowly and well. It tasted fine and none asked for bread or salt—net even Olive, still silent and alone. She accepted the meat, but returned only distant gravity for the teacher's smile.

By now the white blizzard darkness was coming back, but before they slept there was a little piece of boiled veal for each and a little hot broth. It was a more cheerful sleeping time, even a confident one, although in the night they were struck by the diarrhea that Lecia had expected. But that was from the fresh meat and should not last.

By now Lecia could build a coal bed with rotten wood and ashes to hold a fire a long time, even with diamond willows, and so she dressed Maggie's feet, the girl light as a sack of bird bones, and prepared the night fire. For a while Chuck and Eddie kept each other awake with stories of coyote hunts and with plans for another morning of storm, the sixth. The two boys met the day with so much confidence that Lecia had to let them go out into the storm. Eddie, only ten, suddenly became a little old man in his seriousness as he explained their plans carefully. They would make a big brush pile so that they could settle out of the wind and work the fire until they got a whole hindquarter of the calf hacked off. So the teacher watched them go out very full of hope, the hope of meat, one of the half blankets along to drag their prize in over the snow, like great hunters returning.

Bill had looked sadly after the disappearing boot soles, but without complaint. He helped Lecia with the smaller children, washing at the grime of their faces that would never yield except to soap, and took them out into the storm and back while the teacher soaked Maggie's great swollen feet and tried to keep the girl from knowing that the bone ends of her toes could be seen in the suppurating pits of dying flesh. There were holes on the tops of the toes too, along the edges of her feet, and up the heels as high as the ankle. But above there the swelling seemed looser, the red streaks perhaps no farther up the bony legs. Once Bill looked over the teacher's shoulder and then anxiously into her face. Others had chilblains—his own feet swollen from yesterday—but not like this.

"Will she lose—" he started to whisper, but he could not put the rest into words, not with a crippled foot himself.

The air was thick and white with new snow whipped by a northwest wind when Lecia went out for a little wood and to watch for the boys. But they were once more within touching distance before she could see them—very cold and backing awkwardly into the storm through the soft, new drifts, but dragging a whole hindquarter of the calf. It was a lot of meat, and surely the wind must finally blow itself out, the clouds be drained.

By the time Eddie and Chuck were warm they knew they had eaten too much roasted veal while they worked. Next Olive became sick, and Fritz, their deprived stomachs refusing the sudden meat, accepting only the broth. During the night the nausea struck Lecia too, and left her so weak that she could scarcely lift her head all the next day. That night Chuck lost his voice for a while, and Joanie was worse again, her mind full of terrors, the cough so deep, so exhausting that Bill made a little tent over her face with the skirt of his coat to carry steam from a bucket of boiling snow water to her face. Then sometime toward morning the wind turned and cut into the southeast corner of the shelter, crumbling the whole side inward.

The boys crawled out to patch it with brush and snow softened at the fire, Lecia helping dry off the children, as much as she could. Then when they were done and she laid her swimming head down, she heard a coyote's thin, high howl and realized that the wind was dying. Through the smoke hole she saw the running snow like pale windrows of cloud against the sky, and between them stars shining, far pale stars. As one or another awoke, she directed sleepy eyes to look up. Awed, Joanie looked a second time. "You mean they're really stars—?"

"Yes, and maybe there will be sunshine in the morning."

Dawn came early that eighth day, but it seemed that nothing could be left alive in the cold whiteness of the earth that was only frozen scarves of snow flung deep and layered over themselves. The trailing drifts stretched down from the high ridge of hills in the north, so deep that they made a long, sliding slope of it far over the meadow and up the wind-whipped hills beyond, with not a dark spot anywhere to the horizon—not a yucca or fence post or willow above the snow. In the first touch of sun the frozen snow sparkled in the deep silence following a long, long storm. Then out of the hills a lone grouse came cackling over the empty meadow, gleaming silver underneath as she flew, her voice carrying loud in the cold stillness.

But the meadow was not completely empty, for out of a little white mound of drifted willows a curl of smoke rose and spread thin and blue along the hill. There was another sound too, farther, steadier than the cackle of the grouse, a sound seeming to come from all around and even under the feet.

"A plane!" Chuck shouted hoarsely, bursting out into the blinding sunlight.

Several other dark figures crept out behind him into the frosty air, their breath a cloud about them as they stood looking northward. A big plane broke from the horizon over the hills, seeming high up, and then another, flying lower. Foolishly Chuck and Eddie started to shout. "Help! Hello! Help!" they cried, waving their arms as they ran toward the planes, as though to hasten their sight, their coming.

But almost at once the sky was empty, the planes circling and gone. For a long time the boys stared into the broad, cold sky, pale, with nothing in it except wind streaks that were stirring along the ground too, setting feather curls of snow to running.

"Quick! Let's make a big smudge!" Lecia called out, her voice loud in the unaccustomed quiet, and fearful. She threw water on the fire inside, driving smoke out of the hole while the boys set the snowy woodpile to burning.

Before the smoke could climb far, there were planes up over the north hills again, coming fast. Now even Fritz got out into the stinging cold—everybody except Joanie, held back by Lecia, and Olive, who did not move from her place. Maggie was lifted up by the teacher to watch through the smoke hole as something tumbled from the higher plane, came falling down. Then it opened out like the waxy white bloom of the yucca, and settled toward the snow, with several other smaller chutes, bright as poppies, opening behind.

There was shouting and talk outside the shelter and while Lecia was hurrying to get the children into their caps and boots, a man came crawling into the shelter with a bag—a doctor. In the light of the fire and a flashlight he looked swiftly at Joanie and then at Olive, considered her unchanging face, lifted the lids of her eyes, smiled, and got no response. Then he examined the poor feet of Maggie, the girl like a skin-bound skeleton in his first sharp light, her eyes dark and fearful on the man's face.

The doctor nodded reassuringly to Lecia, and smiled down at Maggie.

"You're a tough little girl!" he said. "Tough as the barbed wire you have out in this country. But you're lucky somebody thought to try snow against the gangrene—" He filled a little syringe and fingered cotton as he looked around to divert the child.

"All nine of you alive, the boys say. Amazing! Somebody got word to a telephone during the night, but we had no hope for any of you. Small children lost eight days without food, with fifty inches of snow at thirty-eight below zero. Probably a hundred people dead through the country. The radio in the plane picked up a report that six were found frozen in a car stalled on the highway—not over five miles from town. I don't see how you managed here."

The doctor rubbed the punctured place in the child's arm a little, covered it, smiling into her fearful eyes, as men with a stretcher broke into the front of the shelter.

When they got outside, the air was loud with engine roar, several planes flying around overhead, two with skis already up toward the shelter and a helicopter, hovering like a brownish dragonfly, settling. Men in uniform were running toward the children, motioning where they should be brought.

They came along the snow trail broken by the stretcher men, but walking through it as through the storm. Lecia, suddenly trembling, shaking, her feet unsteady on the frozen snow, was still in the lead, the others behind her, and Chuck once more at the end. Bill, limping awkwardly, carried little Joanie, who clung very close to her brother. They were followed by Calla and Eddie, with Fritz between them, and then the stretcher with Maggie. Only Olive of all the children walked alone, just ahead of Chuck, and brushing aside all help.

There were men running toward the bedraggled, sooty little string now, men with cameras and others, among them some who cried, joyous as children, and who must be noticed, must be acknowledged soon—Olive's father and Dale Stever of the yellow plane—

But for now, for this little journey back from the smoke-holed shelter of snow, the awkward queue stayed together.

The Christmas of the Phonograph Records

Mari Sandoz

The Christmas of the Phonograph Records

IT SEEMS TO ME that I remember it all quite clearly. The night was very cold, footsteps squeaking in the frozen snow that had lain on for over two weeks, the roads in our region practically unbroken. But now the holidays were coming and wagons had pushed out on the long miles to the railroad, with men enough to scoop a trail for each other through the deeper drifts.

My small brother and I had been asleep in our attic bed long enough to frost the cover of the feather tick at our faces when there was a shouting in the road before the house, running steps, and then the sound of the broom handle thumping against the ceiling below us, and father booming out, "Get up! The phonograph is here!"

The phonograph! I stepped out on the coyote skin at our bed, jerked on my woolen stockings and my shoes, buttoning my dress as I slipped down the outside stairs in the fading moon. Lamplight was pouring from the open door in a cloud of freezing mist over the back end of a loaded wagon, with three neighbors easing great boxes off, father limping back and forth shouting, "Don't break me my records!" his breath white around his dark beard.

Inside the house mother was poking sticks of wood into the firebox of the cookstove, her eyes meeting mine for a moment, shining, her concern about the extravagance of a talking machine when we needed overshoes for our chilblains apparently forgotten. The three largest boxes were edged through the doorway and filled much of the kitchen-living room floor. The neighbors stomped their felt boots at the stove and held their hands over the hot lids while father ripped at the boxes with his crowbar, the frozen nails squealing as they let go. First there was the machine, varnished oak, with a shining cylinder for the records, and then the horn, a great black, gilt-ribbed morning glory, and the crazy angled rod arm and chain to hold it in place.

By now a wagon full of young people from the Dutch community on Mirage Flats turned into our yard. At a school program they had heard about the Edison phonograph going out to Old Jules Sandoz. They trooped in at our door, piled their wraps in the leanto and settled along the benches to wait.

Young Jule and James, the brothers next to me in age, were up too, and watching father throw excelsior aside, exposing a tight packing of round paper containers a little smaller than a middle-sized baking powder can, with more layers under these, and still more below. Father opened one and while I read out the instructions in my German-accented fifth-grade country school English, he slipped the brown wax cylinder on the machine, cranked the handle carefully, and set the needle down. Everybody waited, leaning forward. There was a rhythmic frying in the silence, and then a whispering of sound, soft and very, very far away.

It brought a murmur of disappointment and an escaping laugh, but gradually the whispers loudened into the sextet from *Lucia*, into what still seems to me the most beautiful singing in the world. We all clustered around, the visitors, fourteen, fifteen by now, and mother too, caught while pouring hot chocolate into cups, her long-handled pan still tilted in the air. Looking back I realize something of the meaning of the light in her face: the hunger for music she must have felt, coming from Switzerland, the country of music, to a western Nebraska government claim. True, we sang old country songs in the evenings, she leading, teaching us all she knew, but plainly it had not been enough, really nothing.

By now almost everybody pushed up to the boxes to see what there was to play, or called out some title hopefully. My place in this was established from the start. I was to run the machine, play the two-minute records set before me. There were violin pieces for father, among them *Alpine Violets* and *Mocking Bird* from the first box opened; *Any Rags*, *Red Wing*, and *I'm Trying so Hard to Forget You* for the young people; *Rabbit Hash* for my brothers, their own selection from the catalog; and Schubert's *Serenade* and *Die Kapelle* for mother, with almost everyone laughing over *Casey at the Telephone*, all except father. He claimed he could not understand such broken English, he who gave even the rankest westernism a French pronunciation.

With the trail broken to the main bridge of the region, just below our house, and this Christmas Eve, there was considerable travel on the road, people passing most of the night. The lighted windows, the music, the gathering of teams and saddlehorses in the yard, and the sub-zero weather tolled them in to the weathered little frame house with its leanto.

"You better set more yeast. We will have to bake again tomorrow," mother told me as she cut into a *zopf*, one of the braids of coffee cake baked in tins as large as the circle of both her arms. This was the last of five planned to carry us into the middle of holiday week.

By now the phonograph had been moved to the top of the washstand in our parents' kalsomined bedroom, people sitting on the two double beds, on the round-topped trunk and on benches carried in, some squatting on their heels along the wall. The little round boxes stood everywhere, on the dresser and on the board laid from there to the washstand and on the window sills, with more brought in to be played and father still shouting over the music, "Don't break me my records!" Some were broken, the boxes slipping out of unaccustomed or cold-stiffened hands, the brown wax perhaps already cracked by the railroad.

When the Edison Military Band started a gay, blaring galop, mother looked in at the bedroom door, pleased. Then she noticed all the records spread out there, and in the kitchen-living room behind her, and began to realize their number. "Three hundred!" she exclaimed in German, speaking angrily in father's direction, "Looks to me like more than three thousand!"

Father scratched under his bearded chin, laughing slyly. "I added to the order," he admitted. He didn't say how many, nor that there were other brands besides the Edison here, including several hundred foreign recordings obtained through a Swiss friend in New York, at a stiff price.

Mother looked at him, her blue eyes tragic, as she could make them. "You paid nothing on the mortgage! All the twenty-one-hundred-dollar inheritance wasted on a talking machine!"

No, father denied, puffing at his corncob pipe. Not all. But mother knew him well. "You did not buy the overshoes for the children. You forgot everything except your stamp collection, your guns, and the phonograph!"

"The overshoes are coming. I got them cheaper on time, with the guns."

"More debts!" she accused bitterly, but before she could add to this one of the young Swiss, Maier perhaps, or Paul Freye, grabbed her and, against the stubbornness of her feet, whirled her back into the kitchen in the galop from the Edison band. He raced mother from door to stove and back again and around and around, so her blue calico skirts flew out and the anger died from her face. Her eyes began to shine in an excitement I had never seen in them, and I realize now, looking back, all the fun our mother missed in her working life, even in her childhood in the old country, and during the much harder years later.

That galop started the dancing. Hastily the table was pushed against the wall, boxes piled on top of it, the big ones dragged into the leanto. Waltzes, two-steps, quadrilles, and schottisches were sorted out and set in a row ready for me to play while one of the men shaved a candle over the kitchen floor. There was room for only one set of square dancers but our bachelor neighbor, Charley Sears, called the turns with enthusiasm. The Peters girls, two school teachers, and several other young women whom I've forgotten were well outnumbered by the men, as is common in new communities. They waltzed, two-stepped, formed a double line for a Bohemian polka, or schottisched around the room, one couple close behind the other to, perhaps, *It Blew, Blew, Blew*. Once Charley Sears grabbed my hand and drew me out to try a quadrille, towering over me as he swung me on the corner and guided me through the allemande left. My heart pounded in shyness and my home-made shoes compounded my awkwardness. Later someone else dragged me out into a two-step, saying, "Like this: 'one, two; one, two.' Just let yourself go."

Ah, so that was how it was done. Here started a sort of craze that was to hold me for over twenty years, through the bear dance, the turkey trot, the Charleston, and into the Lindy hop. But that first night with the records even Old Jules had to try a round polka, even with his foot crippled in a long-ago well accident. When he took his pipe out of his mouth, dropped it lighted into his pocket, and whirled mother around several times we knew that this was a special occasion. Before this we had never seen him even put an arm around her.

After the boys had heard their selection again, and *The Preacher and the Bear*, they fell asleep on the floor and were carried to their bed in the leanto. Suddenly I remembered little Fritzlie alone in the attic, perhaps half-frozen. I hurried up the slippery, frosted steps. He was crying, huddled together under the feather tick, cold and afraid, deserted by the cat too, sleeping against the warm chimney. I brought the boy down, heavy hulk that he was, and laid him in with his brothers. By then the last people started to talk of leaving, but the moon had clouded over, the night-dark roads winding and treacherous through the drifts. Still, those who had been to town must get home with the Christmas supplies and such presents as they could manage for their children when they awoke in the morning.

Toward dawn father dug out *Sempach*, a song of a heroic Swiss battle, in which one of mother's ancestors fell, and *Andreas Hofer*, of another national hero. Hiding her pleasure at these records, mother hurried away to the cellar under the house for two big hams, one to boil while the Canada goose roasted for the Christmas dinner. From the second ham she sliced great red rounds for the frying pan and I mixed up a triple batch of baking powder biscuits and set on the two-gallon coffee pot. When the sun glistened on the frosted snow, the last of the horses huddled together in our yard were on the road. By then some freighters forced to camp out by an upset wagon came whipping their teams up the icy pitch from the Niobrara River and stopped in. Father was slumped in his chair, letting his pipe fall into his beard, but he looked up and recognized the men as from a ranch accused of driving out bona fide settlers. Instead of rising to order them off the place he merely said "How!" in the Plains greeting, and dropped back into his doze. Whenever the music stopped noticeably, he lifted his shaggy head, complaining, "Can't you keep the machine going?" even if I had my hands in the biscuits. "Play the *Mocking Bird* again," he might order, or a couple of the expensive French records of pieces he had learned to play indifferently in the violin lessons of his boyhood in Neuchatel. He liked *Spring Song* too, and *La Paloma*, an excellent mandolin rendition of *Come ye Disconsolate*, and several German love songs he had learned from his sweetheart, in Zurich, who had not followed him to America.

Soon my three brothers were up again and calling for their favorites as they settled to plates of ham with red gravy and biscuits, Fritzlie from the top of two catalogs piled on a chair shouting too, just to be heard. None of them missed the presents that we never expected on Christmas; besides, what could be finer than the phonograph?

While mother fed our few cattle and the hogs I worked at the big stack of dishes with one of the freighters to wipe them. Afterward I got away to the attic and slept a little, the music from below faint through my floating of dreams. Suddenly I awoke, remembering what day this was and that young Jule and I had hoped father might go cottontail hunting in the canyons up the river and help us drag home a little pine tree. Christmas had become a time for a tree, even without presents, a tree and singing, with at least one new song learned.

I dressed and hurried down. Father was asleep and there were new people in the bedroom and in the kitchen too, talking about the wonder of the music rolling steadily from the big horn. In our Swiss way we had prepared for the usual visitors during the holidays, with family friends on Christmas and surely some of the European homeseekers father had settled on free land, as well as passersby just dropping in to get warm and perhaps be offered a cup of coffee or chocolate or a glass of father's homemade wine if particularly privileged. Early in the forenoon the Syrian peddler we called Solomon drew up in the yard with his high four-horse wagon. I remember him every time I see a picture of Krishna Menon—the tufted hair, the same lean yellowish face and long white teeth. Solomon liked to strike our place for Christmas because there might be customers around and besides there was no display of religion to make him uncomfortable in his Mohammedanism, father said, although one might run into a stamp-collecting priest or a hungry preacher at our house almost any other time.

So far as I know, Solomon was the first to express what others must have thought. "Excuse it please, Mrs. Sandoz," he said, in the polite way of peddlers, "but it seem to uneducated man like me the new music is for fine palace—"

Father heard him. "Nothing's too good for my family and my neighbors," he roared out.

"The children have the frozen feet—" the man said quietly.

"Frozen feet heal! What you put in the mind lasts!"

The peddler looked down into his coffee cup, half full of sugar, and said no more.

It was true that we had always been money poor and plainly would go on so, but there was plenty of meat and game, plenty of everything that the garden, the young orchard, the field, and the open country could provide, and for all of which there was no available market. Our bread, dark and heavy, was from our hard macaroni wheat ground at a local water mill. The hams, sausage, and bacon were from our own smokehouse, the cellar full of our own potatoes, barrels of pickles and sauerkraut, and hundreds of jars of canned fruit and vegetables, crocks of jams and jellies, wild and tame, including buffalo berry, that wonderful, tart, golden-red jelly from the silvery bush that seems to retreat before close settlement much like the buffalo and the whooping crane. Most of the root crops were in a long pit outside, and the attic was strung with little sacks of herbs and poppy seed, bigger ones of dried green beans, sweetcorn, chokecherries, sandcherries, and wild plums. Piled along the low sides of the attic were bushel bags of popcorn, peas, beans, and lentils, the flour stacked in rows with room between for the mousing cat.

Sugar, coffee, and chocolate were practically all we bought for the table, with perhaps a barrel of blackstrap molasses for cookies and brown cake, all laid in while the fall roads were still open.

When the new batch of coffee cake was done and the fresh bread and buns, the goose in the oven, we took turns getting scrubbed at the heater in the leanto, and put on our best clothes, mostly made-over from some adult's but well-sewn. Finally we spread mother's two old country linen cloths over the table lengthened out by boards laid on salt barrels for twenty-two places. While mother passed the platters, I fed the phonograph with records that Mrs. Surber and her three musical daughters had selected, soothing music: Bach, Mozart, Brahms, and the *Moonlight Sonata* on two foreign records that father had hidden away so they would not be broken, along with an a capella *Stille Nacht* and some other foreign ones mother wanted saved. For lightness, Mrs. Surber had added *The Last Rose of Summer*, to please Elsa, the young soprano soon to be a professional singer in Cleveland, and a little Strauss and Puccini, while the young people wanted Ada Jones and *Monkey Land* by Collins and Harlan.

There was stuffed Canada goose with the buffalo berry jelly; ham boiled in a big kettle in the leanto; watercress salad; chow-chow and pickles, sweet and sour; dried green beans cooked with bacon and a hint of garlic; carrots, turnips, mashed potatoes and gravy, with coffee from the start to the pie, pumpkin and gooseberry. At the dishpan set on the high water bench, where I had to stand on a little box for comfort, the dishes were washed as fast as they came off the table, with a relay of wipers. There were also waiting young men and boys to draw water from the bucket well, to chop stove wood and carry it in.

As I recall now, there were people at the table for hours. A letter of mother's says that the later uninvited guests got sausage and sauerkraut, squash, potatoes, and fresh bread, with canned plums and cookies for dessert. Still later there was a big roaster full of beans and sidemeat brought in by a lady homesteader, and some mince pies made with wild plums to lend tartness instead of apples, which cost money.

All this time there was the steady stream of music and talk from the bedroom. I managed to slip in the *Lucia* a couple of times until a tart-tongued woman from over east said she believed I was getting addled from all that hollering. We were not allowed to talk back to adults, so I put on the next record set before me, this one *Don't Get Married Any More, Ma,* selected for a visiting Chicago widow looking for her fourth husband, or perhaps her fifth. Mother rolled her eyes up at this bad taste, but father and the other old timers laughed over their pipes.

We finally got mother off to bed in the attic for her first nap since the records came. Downstairs the floor was cleared and the Surber girls showed their dancing-school elegance in the waltzes. There was a stream of young people later in the afternoon, many from the skating party at the bridge. Father, red-eyed like the rest of us, limped among them, soaking up their praise, their new respect. By this time my brothers and I had given up having a tree. Then a big boy from up the river rode into the yard dragging a pine behind his horse. It was a shapely tree, and small enough to fit on a box in the window, out of the way. The youth was the son of father's worst enemy, the man who had sworn in court that Jules Sandoz shot at him, and got our father thirty days in jail, although everybody, including the judge, knew that Jules Sandoz was a crack shot and what he fired at made no further appearances.

As the son came in with the tree, someone announced loudly who he was. I saw father look toward his Winchester on the wall, but he was not the man to quarrel with an enemy's children. Then he was told that the boy's father himself was in the yard. Now Jules Sandoz paled above his bearding, paled so the dancers stopped, the room silent under the suddenly foolish noise of the big-horned machine. Helpless, I watched father jump toward the rifle. Then he turned, looked to the man's gaunt-faced young son.

"Tell your old man to come in. We got some good Austrian music."

So the man came in, and sat hunched over near the door. Father had left the room, gone to the leanto, but after a while he came out, said his "How!" to the man, and paid no attention when Mrs. Surber pushed me forward to make the proper thanks for the tree that we were starting to trim as usual. We played *The Blue Danube* and some other pieces long forgotten now for the man, and passed him the coffee and *küchli* with the others. He tasted the thin flaky frycakes. "Your mother is a good cook," he told me. "A fine woman."

When he left with the skaters all of father's friends began to talk at once, fast, relieved. "You could have shot him down, on your own place, and not got a day in the pen for it," one said.

Old Jules nodded. "I got no use for his whole outfit, but the music is for everybody."

As I recall now, perhaps half a dozen of us, all children, worked at the tree, looping my strings of red rose hips and popcorn around it, hanging the people and animal cookies with chokecherry eyes, distributing the few Christmas tree balls and the tinsel and candleholders that the Surbers had given us several years before. I brought out the boxes of candles I had made by dipping string in a melted tallow, and then we lit the candles and with my schoolmates I ran out into the cold of the road to look. The tree showed fine through the glass.

Now I had to go to bed, although the room below me was alive with dancing and I remembered that Jule and I had not sung our new song, *Amerika ist ein schönes Land* at the tree.

Holiday week was much like Christmas, the house full of visitors as the news of the fine music and the funny records spread. People appeared from fifty, sixty miles away and farther so long as the new snow held off, for there was no other such collection of records in all of western Nebraska, and none with such an open door. There was something for everybody, Irishmen, Scots, Swedes, Danes, Poles, Czechs as well as the Germans and the rest, something pleasant and nostalgic. The greatest variety in tastes was among the Americans, from *Everybody Works but Father*, *Arkansas Traveler*, and *Finkelstein at the Seashore* to love songs and the sentimental *Always in the Way*; from home and native region pieces to the patriotic and religious. They had strong dislikes too, even in war songs. One settler, a GAR veteran, burst into tears and fled from the house at the first notes of *Tenting Tonight*. Perhaps it was the memories it awakened. Many Americans were as interested in classical music as any European, and it wasn't always a matter of cultivated taste. One illiterate little woman from down the river cried with joy at Rubinstein's *Melody in F*.

"I has heard me talkin' and singin' before," she said apologetically as she wiped her eyes, "but I wasn't knowin' there could be something sweet as that come from a horn."

Afternoons and evening, however, were still the time for the dancers. Finally it was New Year, the day when the Sandoz relatives, siblings, uncles and cousins, gathered, perhaps twenty of them immigrants brought in by the land locater, Jules. This year they were only a sort of eddy in the regular stream of outsiders. Instead of nostalgic jokes and talk of the family and the old country, there were the records to hear, particularly the foreign ones, and the melodies of the old violin lessons that the brothers had taken, and the guitar and mandolin of their one sister. Jules had to endure a certain amount of joking over the way he spent most of his inheritance. One brother was building a cement block home in place of his soddy with his, and a greenhouse. The sister was to have a fine large barn instead of a new home because her husband believed that next year Halley's comet would bring the end of the world. Ferdinand, the youngest of the brothers, had put his money into wild-cat oil stock and planned to become very wealthy.

Although most of their talk was in French, which mother did not speak, they tried to make up for this by complimenting her on the excellence of her chocolate and her golden fruit cake. Then they were gone, hot bricks at their feet, and calling back their adieus from the freezing night. It was a good thing they left early, mother told me. She has used up the last of the chocolate, the last cake of the two twenty-five pound caddies. We had baked up two sacks of flour, forty-nine pounds each, in addition to all that went into the Christmas preparations before the phonograph came. Three-quarters of a hundred pound bag of coffee had been roasted, ground, and used during the week, and all the winter's sausage and ham. The floor of the kitchen-living room, old and worn anyway, was much thinner for the week of dancing. New Year's night a man who had been there every day, all week, tilted back on one of the kitchen chairs and went clear through the floor.

"Oh, the fools!" father shouted at us all. "Had to wear out my floor dancing!"

But plainly he was pleased. It was a fine story to tell for years, all the story of the phonograph records. He was particularly gratified by the praise of those who knew something about music, people like the Surbers and a visitor from a Czech community, a relative of Dvorak, the great composer. The man wrote an item for the papers, saying, "This Jules Sandoz has not only settled a good community of home-seekers, but is enriching their cultural life with the greatest music of the world."

"Probably wants to borrow money from you," mother said. "He has come to the wrong door."

Gradually the records for special occasions and people were stored in the leanto. For those used regularly, father and a neighbor made a lot of flat boxes to fit under the beds, always handy, and a cabinet for the corner at the bedroom door. The best, the finest from both the Edison and the foreign recordings, were put into this cabinet, with a door that didn't stay closed. One warmish day when I was left alone with the smaller children, the water pail needed refilling. I ran out to draw a bucket from the well. It was a hard and heavy pull for a growing girl and I hated it, always afraid that I wouldn't last, and would have to let the rope slip and break the windlass.

Somehow, in my uneasy hurry, I left the door ajar. The wind blew it back and when I had the bucket started up the sixty-five foot well, our big old sow, loose in the yard, pushed her way into the house. Horrified, I shouted to Fritzlie to get out of her way, but I had to keep pulling and puffing until the bucket was at the top. Then I ran in. Fritzlie was up on a chair, safe, but the sow had knocked down the record cabinet and scattered the cylinders over the floor. Standing among them as in corn, she was chomping down the wax records that had rolled out of the boxes, eating some, box and all. Furiously I thrashed her out with the broom, amidst squealings and shouts. Then I tried to save what I could. The sow had broken at least thirty or thirty-five of the best records and eaten all or part of twenty more. *La Paloma* was gone, and *Traumerei* and *Spring Song*; *Evening Star* too, and half of the *Moonlight Sonata* and many others, foreign and domestic, including all of Brahms.

I got the worst whipping of my life for my carelessness, but the loss of the records hurt more, and much, much longer.

Related Readings

Langston Hughes

April Rain Song

With gentle imagery, the poet describes his response to the rain.

Let the rain kiss you.
Let the rain beat upon your head with silver
  liquid drops.
Let the rain sing you a lullaby.

The rain makes still pools on the sidewalk.
The rain makes running pools in the gutter.
The rain plays a little sleep-song on our roof at
  night—

And I love the rain.

Robert Frost

Dust of Snow

Often a small or unimportant event can change one's mood. In this poem, the speaker describes a simple incident and its effect on him.

The way a crow
Shook down on me
The dust of snow
From a hemlock tree

Has given my heart
A change of mood
And saved some part
Of a day I had rued.

Ruth Wallace Brodeur

Snowflake Bentley

Does everyone greet a heavy snowfall with concern? Meet Snowflake Bentley.

WILSON ALWYN BENTLEY lived all his life, from 1865 to 1931, on a farm in Jericho, Vermont, where an average of 120 inches of snow falls each winter. Wilson liked snow so much that he spent his whole life studying it, and because of this, everyone in Jericho called him Snowflake Bentley.

His mother had been a teacher before her marriage, and instead of sending Snowflake to school, she taught him at home. She did a good job, encouraging his curiosity and finding books to answer his many questions. She also managed to buy him an inexpensive microscope, through which he looked closely at flowers, rocks . . . and snowflakes. The beautiful patterns of the flakes intrigued him. He studied them carefully and discovered an ice crystal at the heart of each flake. He tried to draw what he saw, but after 300 drawings he was still dissatisfied, because the snow crystals melted before he could copy all their details on paper.

When he was seventeen, he asked his father for a photomicrograph camera that would take pictures of magnified flakes. The combined microscope and camera cost $100, which was almost as much as the Bentleys earned in one year from selling their crops. But Snowflake and his parents saved all they could, and two years later bought the camera he would use to photograph snowflakes for the next fifty years.

It requires a great deal of skill and speed to take good pictures of snowflakes. The delicate crystals melt away at the slightest breath or the slightest contact with body heat. And even if they don't melt, minor evaporation quickly changes their patterns.

Snowflake Bentley developed a technique that worked well. First he caught some flakes by holding a black wooden tray out in the falling show. Then he brought the tray into his workroom, which was kept at the same temperature as the outside air. Holding his breath and wearing heavy mittens to keep the heat of his hands away from the snow crystals, he quickly examined his catch with a magnifying glass. If a flake looked promising, Bentley touched it very gently at its center with a wooden stick and moved it onto an ice-cold glass microscope slide, stroking it with a feather to flatten it and position it properly. If the crystal still looked good, Snowflake put the glass slide in front of the camera, turned it to face the best light, and took the picture.

Because snow crystals are transparent, they did not show up very well in the finished photograph. So, to make the picture clearer, Snowflake very carefully used a sharp knife to outline each flake on the negative, cutting away all the background film. This increased the beauty of the picture without changing the pattern of the crystals. The whole process required painstaking care, but Snowflake figured it didn't take as much patience for him as it would for others because it gave him such pleasure.

Storm after storm, winter after winter, Bentley caught and photographed crystals. Because most snowflakes are either broken or clumped together, finding a single, undamaged flake was not as easy as it may seem. Some storms were better than others. A "good" storm was one with calm air in which the flakes did not stick together much or get blown about and broken. The winters also varied. In a good season Snowflake might find as many as 300 suitable crystals; in a poor one, maybe only 50 or less. During an especially good storm on 14 February 1928, Snowflake took a record one hundred photographs!

In the thousands of snowflakes he examined, Snowflake Bentley never found any two exactly alike. Even though all of the crystals were based on a hexagonal, or six-sided, pattern, the details of their structures varied endlessly.

Snowflake Bentley also photographed windowpane frost, sleet, ice designs, dew, and mist and studied clouds and storms carefully. His neighbors in Jericho thought it strange for a grown man to spend his time taking pictures of snow and dew, but other people were interested. After Snowflake wrote an article for *Harper's* magazine in 1898, his fame spread, and there was a sudden demand for his photographs.

Tiffany's, the great jewelry store in New York, bought 200 to use as patterns for jewelry designs. Artists, metal workers, silk manufacturers, and craft shops also began using his photos to help plan their designs. Most universities in the country bought collections of his slides. Meteorologists and scientists all over the world studied Snowflake's pictures and read his articles.

Before he died, Snowflake put together a book containing 2,500 of his pictures of snow crystals, frost feathers, and spider webs jeweled with dew. With this book, the man who loved snow left a lasting record of some of the beauty he saw in those tiny, perfect crystals with their intricate designs.

Toni Kim French

They Still Make Country Schoolteachers

In a classroom where students range from five year olds to young teenagers, teacher Toni Kim French finds a joy that she describes here.

5:15 A.M. Alarm clock jolts me out of a deep sleep. That time already? My husband, George, rolls over and says he'll get some coffee started. I think how wonderful he is until he throws back the covers and lets in a massive cold front.

5:30 A.M. Got to pack my lunch. No leftovers today. It'll have to be a sandwich again. I always pack extra food; some kid will forget her lunch at home or won't bring enough.

5:45 A.M. George comes in and reports that we have six inches of new snow and all the horses are fine. Besides me teaching school and George being the anesthetist at the local hospitals, we have a horse-boarding business.

6:15 A.M. I look like I'm going to be gone for a month. An extra coat and shoes. All my books, papers, and lunch. A couple of things I colored and cut out for a new bulletin board. Six bottles of a new paint recipe for art class, and the new soccer ball I picked up last night. A little snow doesn't bother these kids!

6:30 A.M. Country schoolteachers usually beat the snow plows, so it's going to be a slow trip.

6:45 A.M. Made it! First thing I have to do is turn up the furnace and shovel the walks.

7:00 A.M. This is my most productive time of the day! I am the only one here. I check over all lesson plans, review the new algebra equation, make sure all materials are at my fingertips.

7:25 A.M. Alex is here. He always comes early. He won't be far from my side the rest of the day. He just spotted the new soccer ball.

7:30 A.M. I take the new soccer ball and a jump rope away from Alex after they both land in the sink where I'm making a fluoride rinse for the kids. He asks me for the third time if we have to have math today.

7:45 A.M. One of my favorite times of the day. All my kids are here now so I sit down and listen to everything that has happened since yesterday afternoon. Some cows on Kelly's ranch fell through the ice on the river and they spent most of the night trying to save them. Diane gives me a full and complete description of the new 4-H project she started last night. Alex wants to know *why* we have to have math today.

8:00 A.M. We go outside to pledge the flag and all get snow in our shoes. Alex wants to know if we can have math outside today.

8:30 A.M. Everyone is busy working on math. Lee needs extra help so I pull up a chair. Soon Sarah announces she is going to flatten Alex if he pokes her with his pencil one more time. Sarah doesn't make idle threats. Alex sits on the other side of me and whispers that he really thinks my hair is pretty today.

9:00 A.M. In our school, where all different ages and grade levels are in one room, all of the kids get involved in lessons I teach out loud. As the eighth graders and I discuss World War II, the whole room comes alive! Jeff is amazed that anything like that could happen. Diane has tears in her eyes thinking about the victims. I take all the pens and pencils away from Alex. Lee and Scott debate the timing of the U.S. entry into the war. The whole room seems to vibrate;

the kids are coming up with questions and answers on their own. I need to rescue Julia from Alex, who is about to demonstrate what he would do to Hitler if he met him on the street.

10:00 A.M. Recess! We decide to play Fox and Geese. The kids vote to make the course in only geometric shapes. I remind Alex not to throw snowballs or push the younger kids down in the snow.

10:05 A.M. Alex threw three snowballs and pushed Lee down in the snow, so he sits by me on the swings. I want to play Fox and Geese! Alex tells me he doesn't think he has ever seen a nicer pair of snow boots than mine.

11:00 A.M. I make Robin promise that when I am old and in the rest home, she will come read to me; I love to listen to the kids read out loud. Alex interrupts Sarah to ask if we have to have math tomorrow; Sarah glares. Some of the older kids pair up with kindergartners and first graders to read. A good chunk of my monthly paycheck goes toward making sure we always have new books for them to read together.

11:30 A.M. Time for our twice-weekly spelling test. Each grade level has separate spelling words, but with so many grades in one room, there isn't time to give separate tests. The kids say that we don't have spelling tests, but rather spelling dances. I get all the kids ready with paper and pencils. (Whoops! Forgot I took all of Alex's pencils and pens.) Then I do a sort of dance from one grade to another, pronouncing spelling words as I go. There is a certain rhythm to it; the kids sway in their seats. I can pronounce over two hundred spelling words *and* use them in a sentence in under ten minutes. In the end, every kid has the right words for his grade level on his paper.

11:45 A.M. Lunch. Anyone who has ever been to a bidding auction will have an idea of what our room is like at lunchtime. These kids are masters at the swap, trade, bid, and con-your-neighbor lunch hour. As soon as the lunch boxes are opened, a roar goes up. Homemade desserts are the most expensive items. Homemade chocolate cake can go for two pieces of fried chicken, eleven M&M's, three peanut-butter-stuffed celery sticks, and being the pitcher for the next softball game. This ordinary group of easygoing kids turns into ruthless cutthroat wheelers and dealers. I got a slab of banana bread covered with fresh butter for one bag of barbecue potato chips, two pieces of gum, and five butterscotch candies. Costly, but worth it. Alex has to sit by me again. He blew pop out of a straw at Kelly. Alex thinks the color of my sweater makes my eyes pretty.

12:05 P.M. As we get all bundled up to go outside, Julia proclaims that she is too old for these baby games. Julia is almost fourteen, trapped between adult and child. All kids go through this, especially girls. I show her the new soccer ball and she decides maybe she can suffer through one more recess. Kids in western Nebraska learn early how to play any game in the snow, even volleyball. I won't be able to play soccer this recess either. Alex has to stay inside and write apologies to Sarah and Kelly for poking and spitting. That means not only do I supervise playground games, but also stay close to a window so I can keep an eye on Alex. I'm glad I brought an extra coat. Our resident herd of deer comes around to see what the kids are up to.

12:30 P.M. Now it's my turn to read aloud to the kids. I'm reading *Where the Red Fern Grows*. This will be the only time today that I won't have to worry about Alex. He loves to listen to stories and won't move a muscle. Diane has misty eyes, and we haven't even gotten to the sad part yet.

1:00 P.M. I am having a group lesson in English today. We put up huge sheets of newsprint on the walls and are writing down as many homonyms as we can think of. I'll leave the sheets; I'm sure we'll be thinking of more for days to come. Alex has to sit in his chair; poking with pencils again. One of the little girls comes up with "so" and "sew," earning a round of applause. While one of the big boys helps her write them on the newsprint, Alex whispers to me that I am his favorite teacher forever and ever, and maybe I could just think about not having math tomorrow.

1:30 P.M. After science lessons, it's Robin and Alex's turn to rotate the eggs in the incubator. We are waiting for eight chickens and four ducks to hatch. Alex drops a chicken egg on the floor. He feels so bad that he cries. We have an impromptu note-taking session comparing this chicken with a full-term chicken.

2:00 P.M. Julia talks everyone into playing soccer at recess again. The game doesn't last long; the ball hits the barbed-wire fence. We play kick ball the rest of the recess.

2:20 P.M. The kids love the new paint I made; it puffs up as it dries. I am going to have some real masterpieces! Alex is sitting outside the door to paint; he thought Lee could use puffy hair.

2:50 P.M. Just enough time for a quick spelling bee before dismissal. The words are flying fast and furious. Kelly wins on "impervious."

3:05 P.M. Time to go home. A big flurry of coats, lunch boxes, mittens, homework, and books. Alex gives me a big hug as he runs out the door. I try not to look at all the papers waiting for me to check. I clean up the bathrooms and run a broom over the floors. I make a note to myself to remember Sarah's piano recital in town tonight. I find a note from Alex stuck in my lunch box.

> *Dear Mrs. French,*
> *Most of the time you are my best friend.*
> *Can I go home with you someday?*
> *Love, Alex*

5:00 P.M. George has supper started and all the horses, dogs, and cats are fine. Music to my ears!

5:30 P.M. Alex just called to find out if I got his note. I promised I'll bring him home with me someday in the spring—close to the end of the school year.

5:35 P.M. Alex called back to see if I knew exactly when that day would be. We settled on May 7.

8:30 P.M. I smile to myself while reading the local paper. The town teachers are demanding another free period during the day. I wonder if they get bored. They don't have recess or lunch duty; they don't teach their own music, art, or P.E. And they have free periods. Maybe I should move to town. Nah, I'd probably miss Alex.

9:30 P.M. In bed, almost asleep. The phone rings. When I pick up a little voice says, "Mrs. French, do we have to have math tomorrow?"

Nicholasa Mohr

A New Window Display

Nicholasa Mohr writes about friendship and support among a group of neighborhood children.

ON A COLD, bleak Monday morning early in January, Hannibal and Joey walked along the avenue. They were on their way to school. But first, as usual, they stopped in front of the FUNERARIA ORTIZ and looked at the new window display. Sometimes the other kids would be there waiting, but this morning Hannibal and Joey were the first to arrive.

"Man," said Hannibal, "it sure is cold today. Maybe it'll snow."

"I hope so," said Joey. "A whole lotta snow, and we can build some forts. . . . Neat! Huh, Hannibal?"

Hannibal nodded and turned to look at the storefront. "They got a new one today, but it's an old man."

"Again?" Joey asked.

Every Monday, the funeral chapel had a new window display of color photographs showing the recently deceased from different angles, including close-ups. The inscription on every wreath was clearly visible. Hannibal pointed to a large photograph of an older man in a white-satin-lined coffin. His grey hair was neatly combed back, showing a receding hairline. His face was a dark orange, with a pinkish red spot on each cheek, and his lips were a deep purple-red, pushed back into a fixed smile. His eyes were shut. He wore a dark-blue suit and a clean white shirt with a black tie. His hands were folded over the lower part of his chest. They appeared very pale in contrast to his face; almost a greyish white. He wore a plain gold wedding band.

"They got a new one?" someone asked. Hannibal and Joey turned and saw Ramona, Mary, and Casilda.

"Well?" asked Ramona.

"They got an old man," answered Hannibal.

Ramona and the two girls stepped up and looked inside the storefront window. "Again?" Ramona asked.

"Yeah, all they got is old mens," Mary said.

"This guy got a mess of flowers. Look at all them decorations," said Joey. "Let's start reading them, O.K., Hannibal? Or . . . maybe we should wait for Papo and Little Ray." Joey looked at Hannibal, waiting for him to make the final decision.

"He's late, man, and it's cold. I say we start reading," Hannibal replied.

"Maybe we should wait a little bit. You know Papo always has to bring his cousin to school. . . ." Ramona said.

"No!" Hannibal said. "Let's read now." He looked at Ramona defiantly. She shrugged her shoulders.

"To our dear departed—" Hannibal began to read the inscription on one of the wreaths.

"Wait!" Ramona interrupted. "You going first again. You went first the last time."

"I don't remember going first last time," Hannibal said.

"Oh, yes! Right? Ask anybody." Ramona looked at the two girls standing beside her. They both nodded silently.

"What do you think, Joey? Do you think I went first before?"

"I don't remember. I don't think so," Joey replied quickly.

"You see?" Hannibal said to Ramona. "Now let me read!"

Ramona made a face and whispered something.

"What?" asked Hannibal. "What did you say, girl?"

"Nothing," Ramona said, sighing. "Go on."

"To our dear departed Uncle Felix," Hannibal read, "from his loving niece and husband and children, Rojelia and Esteban Martínez, Gilberto, María Patricia and Consuelo."

"Para un gran amigo," Joey read from another wreath, "Felix Umberto Cordero. De la familia Jiménez, 5013 Kelly Street, Bronx, New York."

"From your loving sister, María Elena Martínez and . . ." Ramona took the next turn. Then Mary and Casilda read. It usually went in that order unless Papo and Little Ray were there. Then the girls would be the last ones. Papo was a year younger than the others, and his little cousin was almost two years younger than Papo. Little Ray and his parents had arrived a few months ago from Puerto Rico. They always saved one inscription written in Spanish for him, because he read Spanish better than English.

The children finished reading all the inscriptions. "I guess they are real late, or they ain't coming. We better split or we are gonna be late," said Hannibal.

The group started once more toward school. They walked quickly, feeling the cold wind against their faces and bodies. They turned the corner of Prospect Avenue and headed down Longwood Avenue toward P.S. 39.

Except for a term in the second grade and once in the fourth grade, the group had been in the same classes since kindergarten. This term, they were all in the fifth grade except Papo, who was in the fourth. New in the group, he had become their friend when he moved to the Bronx about a year ago.

Little Ray was always with Papo, who had to look after him. In the four months since he had arrived, he had become the group's favorite. At first he had spoken no English, but now he was almost fluent. He spoke with an accent, which amused the other children, and he would get back at them by correcting their Spanish.

"That's not the way you say it." Little Ray would smile and gently correct them, giving them the proper pronunciation. They would laugh at him, but they could not help being impressed with his ability to speak so well.

"Man . . . Little Ray talks Spanish as good as my grandmother and parents and everybody!" Joey had said.

"Yeah," Ramona agreed. "He sure knows a lot for such a little kid."

The group had become protective of Little Ray, and they soon included him in everything they did. They were always anxious to see and hear his reaction to something different, or new, that he had never seen before.

"Qué fenomenal!" Little Ray would always shout with excitement. Everyone laughed and giggled. After a while, it got to be a game; they would wait for Little Ray to react, and then in unison they echoed, "Phenomenal!"

It was Little Ray's favorite word.

"He may be little but he's got a lotta heart, man. He's phenomenal! . . . And no squealer either," Hannibal had said admiringly, the day that they had all decided to take some potatoes from the vegetable stand in the outdoor market on Union Avenue.

Little Ray and Casilda were assigned to keep the man at the stand busy while the rest of them stuffed their pockets with roasting potatoes. Later, in an empty lot, they skewered the potatoes on long, thin pieces of wood, roasting them over an open fire, waiting for the skin to turn black and the inside soft and hot.

As they ate, a superintendent from one of the nearby tenements came over and began to question Little Ray suspiciously in Spanish. He assured the man, speaking to him in Spanish, that they had all brought the potatoes with them from home. After the man left, they laughed.

"He's the best little kid in El Bronx!" Ramona had said. "Right?"

"Phenomenal!" everyone had shouted in agreement.

Hannibal and Joey rushed on ahead, almost running, and left the girls a few yards behind.

"What do you mean the most flowers?" Hannibal argued with Joey.

"Yeah . . . today that man had the most decorations I seen so far."

"Get out, Joey. Remember the old lady with the wig that time? And the little baby—remember him? Now he had like a hundred decorations."

"Oh yeah, that's right," said Joey. "Do you think that was a real baby?"

"Of course it was! What do you think it was, a dummy?"

"No, but maybe . . . it was like a doll," Joey said.

"It was no doll. Man, Joey, what's the matter with you? Why they gonna give all them flowers to a doll and everything?"

"Well," Joey said. "Anyway, that was no hundred decorations he had. Wasn't even fifty!"

"Well, maybe not a whole hundred. But it was more than fifty and more than that old guy today got. . . . " Hannibal continued trying to convince Joey as they raced to reach school before the late bell rang.

"To Our Dear Departed Brother and Uncle, Carlos Rodríguez . . . " read Hannibal.

"Rest in Peace, Co-Worker. From . . ." read Joey. As usual, they all stood together looking at another new window display. This Monday morning, the weather was quite pleasant, unseasonably warm; and the sun shone brightly. Then it was Papo's turn.

"I'm gonna read the one in Spanish for Little Ray, even though he ain't here today," Papo said. "Querido Esposo, Padre, y Abuelo . . ." he finished reading.

"This guy didn't have so many decorations," said Casilda.

"Yeah, not like the last guy," Joey said. "Look, even the coffin ain't so fancy."

"Yeah."

"Uh huh."

"That's right."

"How is Little Ray?" asked Hannibal. "He ain't been around now for about almost two weeks, right?"

"Yeah . . . well," Papo answered, "I think he's gotta go back to P.R."

"Puerto Rico?" asked Joey. "No kidding?"

"He got something in his chest, like—and they say it's the bad weather here that causes it. It's real bad and he's very sick. They say he gotta go back."

"Aww man, that's too bad!" said Hannibal.

"That's terrible," said Mary.

"When does he gotta leave?" asked Ramona.

"As soon as he gets better, so he can travel," answered Papo. "And he don't like the idea at all, let me tell you. Little Ray says they are very strict down there and that here he is much more free. He likes to hang out with us and play and everything."

"Do you think, Papo, that if he gets really well and all better, that maybe they will let him stay here?" asked Ramona.

"I don't know," Papo shrugged his shoulders. "His parents definitely say he gotta go back and stay with his aunt and uncle down there."

"Too bad," said Casilda. "He's nice."

"He's a real good kid," Hannibal agreed.

"Yeah."

"Uh huh."

The mildness in the air and the bright sun put the children in high spirits. They all walked to school at a slow pace, enjoying the January thaw.

"What a drag," Hannibal said; "going to school on such a day. It feels like springtime. How about cutting today?"

"Get out, Hannibal!" Ramona said quickly. "You better not start that business again and get into trouble. And you better not listen to him, Joey."

"Goody Two-Shoes," Hannibal said, making a face at Ramona.

Ramona stuck her tongue out at Hannibal.

"Whew . . . qué fea . . ." he said good-naturedly. "Ugly as sin." Ramona responded by shrugging her shoulders. Neither of them could really feel angry this morning.

The group strolled along and turned the corner onto Longwood Avenue.

"Hey . . . maybe if the weather changes and it keeps on being warm, they will let Little Ray stay. Then he can come back to school and stick around with us," said Joey.

"I sure hope so," said Papo, smiling. "Except after he gets well, then I hope it snows. He's never really seen snow—he's only seen like a little bit. Like flurries, so far. But I mean a real big storm. This way we could all build a fort, and have snowball fights and everything, you know. . . ."

"Yeah," said Mary, "that's right. Remember, we told Little Ray all about it. He was looking forward to it."

"Right now, let's just hope it stays warm," said Ramona. "That way he can come back and be with us real soon."

"Sure."

"Right."

"Absolutely."

A whole month had passed since Little Ray was buried. Many neighbors had attended the funeral mass. The group did not go, except for Papo. However, the members of the group had gone once to the funeral chapel with their families to pay their respects to Little Ray and his family. By now, things had gone back to normal except that the children no longer met in front of the storefront window of the FUNERARIA ORTIZ on Monday mornings. They just walked past the new window display on their way to school, not looking or stopping. No one ever spoke about it.

This morning, wet snow melted instantly as it hit the concrete pavement and black-tar streets. Hannibal and Joey rushed to school feeling cold and damp. As they approached the funeral chapel, they saw Papo, Ramona, Mary, and Casilda standing right in front of the storefront window.

"Hannibal, Joey—look!" Ramona called out, pointing to the new window display. "Papo told us."

Hannibal and Joey looked inside the storefront window and saw many photographs of Little Ray. There were so many floral wreaths that the small coffin was hardly visible. A large close-up showed him in a powder-blue, silk-lined coffin. His dark curly hair was oiled, combed and parted on the side. Little Ray's eyes were shut and his face was colored a light pink. Each cheek had a dark pink spot. His lips were bright orange and slightly parted. He looked like he was smiling, dreaming a pleasant dream. He wore his dark-blue First Holy Communion suit, with a white satin sash tied on his left sleeve, a white starched shirt, and a dark-blue tie. His small pale hands held a white missal and a set of white rosary beads with a gold cross.

"I thought we should stop. . . ." Papo hesitated. "My parents told me last night, and I figured that it would only be right . . . for us to come here. For Little Ray."

The group remained silent for a while.

"Wow!" Hannibal said, breaking the silence. "He sure looks different, don't he?"

"Yeah," Joey said. "I never even seen him with his hair combed before. He even looks healthy, like he got a sunburn."

"My father says they do a good job here," said Papo, nodding. "They made him look like he was making his Communion again. They made everything perfect."

"He looks nice," Mary said.

"Oh . . . yeah, he does," said Casilda. "Like a little angel. Right?"

"He sure does." Ramona nodded.

"Now," Hannibal said. "He's the one that got the most flowers of anybody I ever seen!"

"That's right!" said Joey. "Even more than that little baby."

"Uh huh."

"The most!"

"Absolutely."

The children stood quietly and looked into the storefront window. The wet snow continued to fall. They were all damp and chilly, but no one moved. After a while, Papo asked, "Do you think we should read?"

The children looked at each other and shrugged. Then everyone turned to look at Hannibal.

"O.K.," Hannibal said, "who's gonna go first?" Everyone was surprised. Hannibal had never asked anyone to be first before.

"You go first," said Ramona. "Like you always do." Hannibal opened his mouth to protest, but Ramona stared at him and, folding her arms, said quickly, "Go on!" Hannibal read slowly.

"To the Santiago family in their Hour of Bereavement . . ." He read on, looking at Joey when he finished.

"Beloved Son, Ramon Luis . . ." Joey read.

Each took a turn. There were so many wreaths that they went twice around, and Hannibal and Joey had to read a third time. Finally they were all finished.

"I still miss him, you know," Papo said. "I never even minded taking care of him . . . like he was no bother. Other little kids, man, you know, they can really be pests. But not him."

"He was really a good kid," said Hannibal.

"It's kinda funny, because like I know he's not gonna be around no more, yet like I can't believe he's gone." Papo paused for a moment, then continued, "Anyway, my parents ordered some of them pictures and this way we can remember him like he looked."

They walked silently toward school. It began to snow harder, and large snowflakes stuck to the pavement, piling up. Areas of sidewalk were covered by a soft white blanket. The children felt the soft crunch under their feet, so different from the familiar hard concrete.

"Hey!" yelled Joey. "We got us a real big snowstorm!"

"Hurray!"

The group shouted, sliding and turning.

"Oh, boy, imagine if Little Ray were here and seen this!" said Papo excitedly.

"Oh man! He would be so happy!" Hannibal smiled. "And we all know what he would say. . . . "

"Phenomenal!" everyone shouted.

Isaac Bashevis Singer
Translated by Joseph Singer

A Hanukkah Eve in Warsaw

In this story, Singer shares with readers the richness and beauty of a holy day and the strength of family love.

1

FOR TWO WEEKS NOW WARSAW—and perhaps all Poland—had lain in the grip of a cold spell the likes of which hadn't been seen in years. But I, a child not yet seven, kept going to cheder early each morning. We—my parents, my older brother Joshua, my sister Hindele, my younger brother Moshe, and I—lived at 10 Krochmalna Street and the cheder was located at 5 Grzybowska Street. In the mornings, an assistant to the teacher came to take me to cheder, and he brought me home again in the evenings. To keep me from freezing on the way, Mother wrapped me in two woolen vests, two pairs of socks, and gloves. She stuck a hood on my head which covered my red hair and earlocks; when I looked in the mirror I couldn't recognize myself and stuck my tongue out at the stranger.

The long winter night passed full of dreams. Now I dreamed I was an emperor, and now a beggar. An old crone of a gypsy snatched me and locked me in a cellar. I also dreamed that it was summer and that I was strolling with Shosha, the daughter of our neighbor Bashele, in a garden full of blooming flowers and singing birds. I sailed a boat on the Vistula but soon pirates captured me and spirited me off to Madagascar to be sold into slavery. My dreams blended with my fantasies and with the tales I had heard from my mother or read in storybooks.

That winter morning was a cold but sunny one. The sky above the rooftops loomed a light blue. Although our oven was heated with wood and coal, frost patterns had formed on our windows overnight. They resembled trees, not those common to Poland, but rather the date palms and fig and carob trees the Bible said grew in the Land of Israel.

Normally, I stayed at the cheder until nightfall, but that day was the eve of Hanukkah and I was scheduled to come home earlier than usual. I liked Hanukkah—the only holiday that came in the winter. In the evening, right after services, Father would bless the Hanukkah candles, Mother would fry potato pancakes, I would get a tin dreidel and money for the holiday. I could hardly wait to get home.

Before I left the house, Mother gave me a paper bag containing bread and butter, cheese, and an apple. This was to be my second breakfast. The assistant teacher took my hand and led me down the stairs into the street. Mother warned him not to let go of me. In such a large city a child could easily get lost. The streets were filled with sleighs and I was liable to be run over, God forbid. I was ashamed that my mother was such a worrier. She came from a small town and provincial people imagined all kinds of dangers in the big city. I had come to Warsaw when I was three and I considered myself a city boy. I could have gone to cheder by myself; I didn't have to be escorted there. I envied the other children my age who went to cheder alone. It seemed to me they laughed at me for being escorted like a baby.

God in heaven, how different the street looked today, all covered by the fresh snow that had fallen overnight! The sleighs and pedestrians hadn't yet managed to trample it, and it glared beneath the sun, reflecting dazzling crystals of every color of the rainbow. One solitary tree grew on our street and its naked branches were covered with frost. They reminded me of the arms of a huge Hanukkah candelabrum. Sleighs rode by with bells on horses' collars jingling. The animals' nostrils exuded steam. Cushions of snow lay on roofs and balconies. The whole world had turned white, rich, and dreamlike.

2

Coming to cheder was for me a daily trial. The other pupils quickly made friends with one another. They conducted all kinds of secret business transactions among themselves. One boy gave another a silver button and got a gold button in exchange. Quietly, so that the teacher wouldn't see, they traded pencils, pens, and sometimes chocolates and cookies they brought from home. Most of the students were sons of storekeepers or factory owners and were already little businessmen themselves. Their parents lived in the wealthier streets. Some of the students brought a different toy to cheder each day—lead soldiers, whistles, trumpets. One boy had a pen with a peephole. When you looked into it you saw Cracow. Another boy had a music box. When you turned the key it played a tune. One boy had a real watch. Most of them had black hair, and some were blond, but no one in the cheder besides me had hair as red as fire. Nor did anyone else wear such long earlocks. I was a rabbi's son and my parents dressed me in the old-fashioned style. I had been raised in Warsaw, but I looked like a yokel. The boys laughed at me and my small-town costumes. They even mocked the way I pronounced some words in Yiddish. Besides, they couldn't do any trading with me. I brought nothing to cheder except my Pentateuch.

I always felt ashamed when I came to cheder, and I often prayed to God to let me grow up faster so that I could be through with being a child. But I had some satisfaction, too. All children love to hear stories and I had acquired the reputation of a storyteller. I was also able to add my own fantasies to the stories we read in the Pentateuch. At Hanukkah time the teacher studied with us the section that dealt with Joseph and his brothers. I retained the meaning of the Hebrew words better than many of the other children, and I repeated the tale as if I had been there in person. Joseph's dreams became my dreams. The brothers envied me and sold me into slavery to the Ishmaelites, who in turn sold me to the Egyptians. Potiphar had me imprisoned, and later I became viceroy to Pharaoh. Jacob, Joseph, the other tribes, Laban, Rachel, Leah, Bilhah, Zilpah were all as close and familiar to me as my own mother and father, as our neighbor Bashele and her daughter, Shosha, with whom I carried on an unspoken love affair. As I sat in cheder over the Pentateuch, I yearned for her and her childish words, which held a thousand delights for me . . .

By three o'clock we had concluded our portion and the teacher, Reb Moshe Yitzchok, a patriarch of eighty, put down the pointer and the hare's leg with the thong that he used to whip bad pupils, and told us to go home.

The assistant teacher came up to me and began, with hesitation, "You always say that you could find your way home by yourself. Is this true?"

"Yes, it's true."

"You wouldn't get lost?"

"Lost? I could get home in the middle of the night!"

"I've got something to do and I don't have the time to take you home. Can I trust you to get home by yourself?"

"Yes, yes . . ."

"You won't tell your parents?"

"Tell? No, never!"

"Is that a promise?"

"I swear it on my ritual fringes."

"You don't have to swear on your ritual fringes."

"I wouldn't say anything even if they should kill me."

"Well, all right. Go straight home and don't stop along the way. You'll tell them I took you to the gate of your house."

"Yes."

The assistant teacher helped me put on my overcoat, the hood, the gloves, the galoshes. The other boys laughed and made fun of me. They called me a sissy, a mama's boy, a little rabbi, a spoiled brat. One of them showed me his tongue, another made the sign of the fig. A third said, "He is Joseph from the Bible. His father will make him a coat of many colors. . ."

3

I wanted to boast to the boys that I was going home all by myself, but the assistant teacher apparently guessed my intentions, for he put his finger to his lips.

I went out into the street, and for the first time I felt like a grownup. How short the days were in winter! It was just a quarter past three but the sky was already a dusky blue. Several cheder boys were sliding on the frozen gutter, trying to make the figure called "little shoemaker." When they saw me walking alone, they began to yell and make faces as if about to chase me. One of them threw a snowball at me. I moved away from them quickly. They only waited for a chance to start a fight and show off their strength. On Gnoyna Street I stopped in front of a shop window. Although the store belonged to a Jew, it sold the globes, bells, lights, and spangles Gentiles drape on Christmas trees. A man holding a long pole lit the gas streetlights. Women sat in doorways, on boxes and on footstools, hawking their wares—potato cakes, hot chick-peas, hot lima beans, bagels, oil cakes. The smells these delicacies sent out were delicious. I began to fantasize what I would do if I had a million rubles. I would buy all these goodies and make a feast for Shosha. We would munch on chocolate, halvah, tangerines, and take a ride in a sleigh. I would stop going to cheder and have a rabbi tutor me at home.

I was so preoccupied with my reveries I didn't notice that it had started snowing. A dense snow began to fall, dry and grainy as salt. My eyes crusted over. The street gaslights became covered with snow and their shine turned orange, blue, green, violet. This wasn't merely snow but snow mixed with sleet. Chunks of ice fell from the sky and a strong wind began to blow. Maybe the world was coming to an end? It seemed to me that there was thunder and lightning.

I started to run and I fell several times. I picked myself up, and to my alarm I saw that I had strayed into some other street. Here, the streetlights weren't gas but electric. I saw a trolley that wasn't drawn by horses. The rod extending from its roof to the wires overhead sprayed bluish sparks. A fear came over me—I was lost! I stopped passersby and asked them directions, but they ignored me. One person did answer me, but in Polish, a language I had never learned. I could barely keep from crying. I wanted to turn back to where I had come from, but apparently I only strayed farther away. I passed brightly illuminated stores and a building with balconies and columns like some royal palace. Music was playing upstairs, and below, merchants were clearing away their goods from the stalls. The wind scattered kerchiefs, handkerchiefs, shirts, and blouses, and they whirled in the air like imps. That which I had always feared had apparently happened—the evil spirits had turned their wrath on me.

Now the wind thrust me forward, now it dragged me back. It blew up the skirt of my coat and tried to lift me in the air. I knew where the gale sought to carry me—to Sodom, to beyond the Mountains of Darkness, to Asmodeus's castle, to Mt. Sair, where the ground is copper and the sky is iron. I wanted to cry out to God, to utter some prayer or incantation, but my mouth had gone numb and my nose was stiff as wood. The cold penetrated through my coat, and through both vests. My eyelids became swollen and I could no longer see in the white maelstrom.

Suddenly I heard a shrill clanging and shouts. Someone sprang and, seizing me from behind, half dragged, half carried me off. Was this a demon, a wraith? A man in a long coat and a black beard turned white from the snow and frost shouted at me in rage, "Where are you running? Where do you creep to? You just missed being run over by the trolley car."

I wanted to thank him but I couldn't utter a word.

The man asked, "Who lets a child out in such a blizzard? You have no parents?"

I still don't know why, but I said, "No, I'm an orphan."

"An orphan, eh? Who do your live with?"

"My grandfather."

"Where does your grandfather live?"

I gave a false address—13 Krochmalna Street.

"What are you doing here if you live at 13 Krochmalna? Got lost, eh?"

"No."

"Where were you going?"

"I wanted to say the mourner's prayer," I replied, astounded by my own lie.

"No synagogues or prayerhouses on Krochmalna? I see that you're lost. Come, I'll take you back."

He took my hand and led me along.

He asked, "What does your grandfather do? How does he make a living?"

"A porter," I said. The words issued from my mouth as if on their own.

"An old man a porter? He's still got the strength to carry? You hungry?"

"No. Yes."

"Wait, I'll get you something."

We walked only a few minutes. I had assumed I had strayed far from Krochmalna, but suddenly I saw it again. I wanted to get away from the man and my lies, but he held me firmly by the hand. He said, "Don't try to run away, boy. Poverty is no disgrace."

He led me into a restaurant. I had passed this restaurant earlier that day. Summer and winter a cloud of steam hovered inside it, and it always smelled of fried onions, garlic, meat, soup, beer. At night music was played there. I once heard my mother say that they served food that wasn't strictly kosher and that it was patronized by gangsters, thieves, the rabble. One boor there had bet that he could eat a whole roast goose. He was about to swallow the last bite when he got sick and had to be taken to the hospital. Now I was there myself. The floor was tiled in white and black like a checkerboard. Burly men and fat women sat at tables covered in red. Some ate boiled beef, others drank beer from mugs. Many gaslights were flashing. Waiters in white aprons carried huge trays with dishes above the diners' heads. There were other rooms here; from one came the sounds of singing, an accordion, hands clapping.

The man with me couldn't find a table. He stood with me in the crush and spoke to everyone and to no one: "An orphan. Nearly got run over. Hungry, poor thing. Half frozen. Give him something to eat. It's a good deed!"

He begged in my behalf. Again I tried to slip away from him, but he held me fast. The walls here were covered with red tapestries and hung with mirrors, so that I saw myself many times over.

A stout woman came up and asked my benefactor, "Why are you holding this boy? Has he done something?"

"Done something? He's done nothing. A poor orphan and hungry."

"An orphan? He's our rabbi's son. His parents are living. I saw his mother this very day at the butcher's."

"Eh? But he told me he was an orphan and that his grandfather is a porter—"

"A porter? Has he gone mad?"

The man apparently grew so confused that he let go of my hand. I dashed off. In a moment I was outside again.

4

I barely recognized the street. My brother Joshua had often spoken of the North Pole and the fact that the nights there lasted six months. Krochmalna Street now appeared to me like the North Pole. Huge mounds of snow had fallen. Whole towers and mountains had formed on the gutter. The pedestrians sank into the snowy depths. Misty trails extended from the street lamps. The sky hung low, reflecting a violet tinge with no moon or stars showing. I tried to run, fearing the man would catch me and punish me for my lies. I had committed so many sins! My parents would soon discover that I had deceived the man and posed as an orphan. They would also learn that the assistant teacher had let me walk home alone and that I had gotten lost. The boys at the cheder would have something to mock at and would make up new nicknames for me. The assistant teacher would become my enemy.

Suddenly I recalled a story my brother Joshua had told me about a boy who had been sent on a Passover night to open the door for the prophet Elijah and had vanished. Years later he came home a grown man and a professor. He had walked from the town where his parents lived to Warsaw, and then on to Berlin. Rich people there had helped him obtain an education. That's what I would have to do, too—run away from home! I would read all the books about the sun, the moon, the stars. I would learn how mountains, rivers, oceans, and the North Pole had formed. My father had one answer for everything—God had created it all. He wanted me to study only religious books. But the worldly books obviously had many other explanations.

Joshua often spoke about science. He said that a cheder education left one ignorant. He spoke of a telescope through which you could see the mountains and craters of the moon. Since we lived in Warsaw, I could proceed straight to Berlin. I knew that a train left for Germany from the Vienna depot. I would simply follow the tracks till I came to Berlin. But what would my parents do if I didn't come home? And what about Shosha? I would miss her terribly. A strange notion came to me: maybe Shosha would run away with me. In storybooks I often read of boys and girls who left home together on account of love. True, these were grownups, but I loved Shosha. I thought of her during the day and I dreamed about her at night. We would study together in Berlin, and when I became a professor, we would marry and come back to Warsaw. Everyone on Krochmalna Street would come out to greet us. My mother and Shosha's mother would weep and embrace. By then, everyone would have forgotten the silly things I had done today. The cheder boys who now pushed me around and called me names would come to me to teach them science and philosophy. . .

I had reached the gate of 10 Krochmalna Street, but instead of going home I went to Shosha's. I had to talk to her! In my mind I prayed to God that she would be home alone. Her father worked in a store and her mother often went to shop at the bazaar or to gossip with her sister. This time luck was with me. I knocked and Shosha opened. She seemed frightened by me and she said, "Oh, just look at you! White as a snowman."

It was warm in Shosha's kitchen and I promptly began telling her of my plans. She sat down on a footstool. She was blond, blue-eyed, and wore her hair in braids. She was exceptionally pale. Although she was my age, she was like a child of five. She played with dolls and got poor grades at the Polish school she attended. She couldn't read or figure properly. I now suggested that she accompany me to Berlin. Shosha heard me out calmly, then asked, "What will we eat?"

I was dumbfounded. I had completely forgotten that a person had to eat.

After a while I said, "We'll take food from home."

"And where will we sleep?"

I didn't know what to say. The trip to Berlin would undoubtedly take weeks. In the summer you could sleep outdoors, but in the winter it would be too cold. For a moment I wondered at my own stupidity and at Shosha's wisdom. Suddenly the door opened and my mother came in with my sister, Hindele, close behind her.

Hindele exclaimed, "There he is, Mama! What did I tell you?"

Mother stared at me in confusion. "So there you are. . . . We've been searching for you two hours. I thought, who knows *what* happened. . ." And all at once she erupted, "Unfaithful child!"

I knew full well the meaning of this expression—a faithless son and a rebellious one. According to the law of the Pentateuch, I should be turned over by my parents to the town elders, who would condemn me to be stoned. An interrogation was forthcoming and I had no excuses ready.

My sister said, "We were waiting for you for the blessing of the Hanukkah candles."

"Where were you all this time? Didn't the assistant teacher bring you?" Mother asked.

"Yes, he brought me."

"When? You've been sitting here two hours?"

"He just came in this second," Shosha said.

"Why were you running around in such a storm? Why did you come here instead of home?"

"He wants us to follow the train tracks . . ." Shosha said, not intending to inform, but simply because she didn't understand the significance of it all.

My sister began to laugh. "He wants to run away with little Shosha! He's carrying on a love affair with her!"

"Don't laugh, Hindele, don't laugh!" Mother said. "The boy is making me sick!"

"Look at him! White as chalk!" my sister observed.

"Come!" Mother said.

She grabbed me by the collar and led me away. I anticipated a severe punishment, but when Father saw me, he only smiled and said, "I'm waiting for you with Hanukkah candles. I have a gift for you, too."

"He's got no gifts coming," Mother exclaimed. "He was outside in the cold the whole time. You didn't even ask where I found him!" she reproached Father. "At our neighbor's, at Bashele's!"

"Who is this Bashele?" Father asked.

"Abraham Kaufman's wife."

"What was he doing there?"

"They have a girl, some little fool, and he wants to run away with her."

Father arched his brows. "Oh, so? Well, it's Hanukkah. I don't want to spoil the holiday."

In honor of the holiday Father had donned his velvet housecoat. Our ceiling lamp was lit. The Hanukkah candelabrum stood ready. A red candle—the so-called sexton—rested in its holder. Father poured in olive oil and fussed with the wick. He made the benediction and lit a candle with the "sexton." Father's red beard glowed like fire. He took a prayer book with wooden covers from his pocket. It had a carving of the Western Wall on the front cover and one of the Cave of Machpelah on the back.

He said, "This prayer book comes from the Land of Israel."

"From the Land of Israel?"

I took the prayer book with joy and trepidation. I had never before held an object that stemmed from this distant and sacred land. It seemed to me that this prayer book exuded the scent of figs, dates, carob beans, cloves, cedar. All the stories from the Scriptures suddenly came to mind: of Sodom, of the Dead Sea, of Rachel's Tomb, of Joseph's dreams, of the ladder the angels climbed up to and down from heaven, as well as of King David, King Solomon, the Queen of Sheba.

My sister, Hindele, said, "Why does he get a gift?" And she added, "The worst dog gets the best bone."

"You'll see that the boy will cause us shame and disgrace!" Mother complained. "I don't believe that the assistant teacher brought him here at all. He always brings him into the house."

"Well, it's a holiday, a holiday!" Father said half to us, half to himself.

"You'll spoil him so, he'll become completely wild," Mother warned.

"With the Almighty's help, he'll grow up a decent man," Father said. He turned to me. "Pray from this book. Everything that comes from the Land of Israel is holy. This Wall is a remnant of the Holy Temple, which the evildoers demolished. The Divine Presence reigns there forever. Jews sinned; that's why the Temple was destroyed. But the Almighty is all-merciful. He is our Father and we are His children. God willing, the Messiah will come and we'll all go back to our homeland. A fiery Temple will descend upon Jerusalem. The dead will be resurrected. Our grandfathers, grandmothers, great-grandfathers, and all the generations will live again. The light of the sun will be seven times brighter than now. The saints will sit with crowns upon their heads and study the secrets of the Torah."

"Mama, the potato pancakes are getting cold," Hindele said.

"Oh, yes!"

And my mother and sister went back to the kitchen.

"Where did you go?" Father asked. "It's freezing outside. You might have caught cold, God forbid. You'd be better off glancing into a holy book."

"Papa, I'd like to study science," I said, astounded at my own words.

"Science? What kind of science?"

"Why summer is warm and winter is cold. How high is the moon and what happens up on the stars. How deep is the earth and how tall is the sky. Everything . . . everything. . . "

"All knowledge is contained in the Torah," Father replied. "Every letter of the Torah conceals countless secrets and infinite depth.

Those who study the cabala acquire more truth than all the philosophers."

"Papa, teach me the cabala."

"Cabala isn't for boys. You may not study the cabala until you're thirty."

"I want it now!"

"Wait. You're still a child. What do you do there at the neighbors'? Who is that little girl? Since she's a fool, what do you need with her?"

"She is *not* a fool."

"Eh? Then what is she?"

"She is good. The boys at cheder call me names, but she is nice to me. When we grow up, I want to marry her," I said, baffled by my own words. It was as if a dybbuk had spoken out of me and I was overcome with fear.

Father smiled, but he promptly grew earnest. "Everything comes from heaven. It's said that forty days before a person is born, an angel in heaven calls out: 'This one's daughter will marry that one's son.' What's this girl's name?"

"Shosha."

"Shosha? I had an Aunt Shosha. She was my aunt and your great-aunt."

"Where does she live?"

"Aunt Shosha? In heaven, in Paradise. She was a saint. She would go to the Belz rabbi and he would place her in a seat of honor. In her old age she went to the Land of Israel and there she died. Oh, I have another gift for you, a dreidel."

The door opened and Mother and Hindele brought in the potato pancakes. During the brief time Mother had been in the kitchen her face had relaxed. My sister was smiling. I showed Mother the shining new dreidel and she gave me a sharp glance.

"You got lost, eh?"

I wanted to deny it, but I could not speak from too much happiness. Besides, she knew everything, just like a prophetess. She often read my mind. Her big gray eyes seemed to say, "I know all your antics but I love you anyhow."